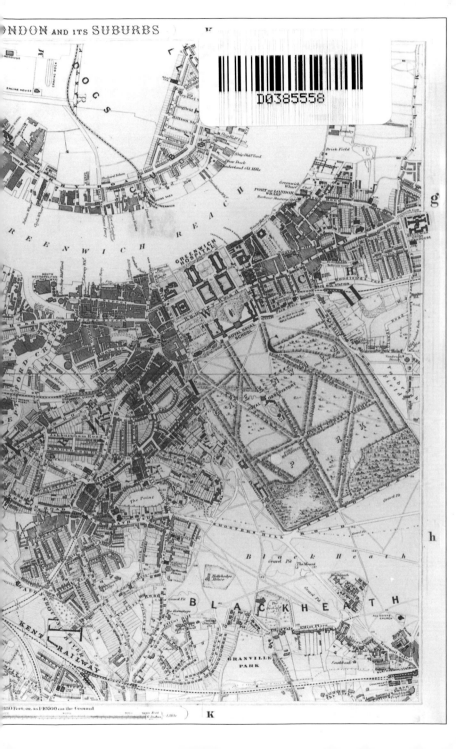

GREENWICH

Charles A. [signature]
December 1999

Also by Charles Jennings

Up North: Travels Beyond the Watford Gap
People Like Us: A Season Among the Upper Classes
Father's Race: A Book About Paternity

GREENWICH

*The Place Where Days
Begin and End*

CHARLES JENNINGS

LITTLE, BROWN AND COMPANY

A *Little, Brown* Book

First published in Great Britain in 1999
by Little, Brown and Company

Copyright © Charles Jennings 1999

A CIP catalogue record for this book
is available from the British Library.

ISBN 0 316 85152 3

Typeset in Goudy by M Rules
Printed and bound in Great Britain by
Clays Ltd, St Ives plc

UK companies, institutions and other organisations wishing
to make bulk purchases of this or any other book published
by Little, Brown should contact their local bookshop or
the special sales department at the address below.
Tel 0171 911 8000. Fax 0171 911 8100.

Little, Brown and Company (UK)
Brettenham House
Lancaster Place
London WC2E 7EN

CONTENTS

GREENWICH

MARITIME I

I F THERE'S one scene that epitomises Greenwich, that does duty for it in the guidebooks and stands for the whole place in people's imaginations, it's the view of the Royal Naval College from the north side of the River Thames. On the north side, you're on the tongue of land known as the Isle of Dogs, part of the London Borough of Tower Hamlets. There's a little rectangle of grass, known as Island Gardens, created by the London County Council in 1895 to ensure that there would always be a place on which you can stand and view that aspect of the college, as viewed by Canaletto himself and immortalised in his famous painting of the Greenwich Hospital (as the Naval College then was), done in 1750. This is the picture which shows Wren's last masterpiece bathed in a lustrous pink sunset, a man-o'-war dramatically beached on the north shore, while a score of skiffs and sailboats busy themselves on the placid bosom of the river. The Greenwich Hospital itself sits securely in the middle of the scene, pink and blue sky above, olive waters below, presiding over the display with a kind of benign detachment. This is the quintessence of eighteenth-century order and reasoned calm, a building whose values impart themselves to everything around it. It is a beautiful and serene painting, a hymn of praise to the virtues of the Age of Reason.

Today, however, at the start of the twenty-first century, the mood is rather different, even though the building itself has hardly changed. For a start, the Thames is not the calm but lively summertime lake that appears in Canaletto's riverscape. Indeed, it very rarely is at this point: once past the Houses of Parliament further upriver, the Thames becomes notoriously choppy, even in fine weather. As it heads out towards the estuary, passing the twists and loops of Limehouse, Millwall and North Greenwich, it usually works itself up into a grey, squally mass, to the surprise and irritation of sailboats making their way into the quiet haven of St Katharine's Dock, by Tower Bridge. Greenwich, in other words, is usually viewed across an expanse of chilly wavelets, often with an easterly wind blowing in from the sea to heighten the effect.

What's more, all the lively business of the sailboats and skiffs – or indeed, of any kind of boat – has vanished. A hundred years ago, this stretch of the river would have been black with working vessels, bringing goods and materials up into the docks, to say nothing of the tugs, lighters, ferryboats and miscellaneous craft supporting them. Paddle-steamers ran constantly from Greenwich Pier, while sailing barges – great gaff-rigged things – worked on the river at Greenwich until the Second World War. As one Hipployte Taine wrote, in the 1870s: 'From Greenwich the river is nothing but a street a mile broad and upwards, where ships ascend and descend between two rows of buildings, interminable rows of dull red, in brick and tiles bordered with great piles stuck in the mud for mooring vessels . . . to the West rises an inextricable forest of yards, of masts, of rigging.'

But not now. If you wait long enough, a ferryboat with sightseers on board will make its way past, as will a Port of London Authority launch, or, just occasionally, a dredger. But not much more than that. The river is pretty silent, nowadays; Canaletto's festive activity lost to an unimaginable past.

It's a feeling which extends to the encompassing shores, too. Where Canaletto's picture cuts off the bank to east and west of the hospital buildings, we can see the whole surrounding region. To the west stand the glass dome of the Greenwich Foot Tunnel, the masts of the *Cutty Sark*, the great nineteenth-century tea clipper, dry-docked by the waterfront, followed by an expanse of council flats edging into neighbouring Deptford. To the east is the Trafalgar Tavern, a Regency-style stuccoed building, dating from 1837, and, like the *Cutty Sark*, at least in keeping with the spirit of the place. But beyond that, echoing the drab realities of Deptford's flats, is a huge power station, built in 1906 by the

London County Council to provide power for the then-new electric tram network. Four chimneys stand bolt upright in the sky, while a simply enormous fuel jetty sticks out into the river. The whole edifice is quite big enough not just to challenge the domes and columns of the Naval College, but to overwhelm them completely. And this is followed in turn by a long graceless sweep of cranes and terminal buildings along the Blackwall Reach, subsiding into the water and the estuary beyond. You are aware that this is, indeed, a long way from the centre of London – six miles at least – and that just round the next bend in the river you will come to the real estuarial landscape: one of flats and marshes, looming factory buildings, power stations, grain silos and oil terminals, an immense, bleak flatness, finally spreading out into the deep water moorings at Tilbury and Canvey Island and then to the open sea. You feel separated from the heart of things, very much on the outer fringes.

Seen in this context, the Naval College is strange and misplaced; not reasoned and inevitable, as Canaletto painted it. It looks like a cross between Buckingham Palace and St Paul's Cathedral stuck in an outermost suburb, with the Queen's House – designed by Inigo Jones in 1616, for Queen Anne of Denmark, consort of James I – appearing pale and lost, bracketed between the monumental designs of Wren's building. So potent is the symmetry of the place, aided by a 1930 statue of General Wolfe at the top of Greenwich Park, that you feel irrationally cheated that the meridian line doesn't run through the centre of the composition, as everything else appears to. Because the Royal Observatory buildings refuse to fit in: they make a knot of red and brown brickwork on the skyline, whose off-centredness (the French would have knocked it down and rebuilt it in the right place) either annoys, or redeems the scene with an essentially humane, essentially English, reduction of formality.

But why is it all here? Why is this tremendous collection of buildings on a draughty bend of the river, with only the bleak Isle of Dogs shoreline (now punctuated by the tower of Canary Wharf, also off centre) to look at? What caused this unique image of Greenwich to come about? Why *Greenwich*?

While London was being founded – and, indeed, named – by the Romans who established it at some time around AD 60, Greenwich was just a fishing community on a reach in the lower river. The first bridge across the Thames was miles further up, built across the sandbanks at Southwark: the first concentration of power and business, the first port, was on the north bank in the new city of Londinium. Greenwich was mainly of interest to the Roman occupiers insofar as it sat close to Watling Street, the Roman road leading from London to Dover (nowadays, the unglamorous Shooters Hill Road), passing over the area of Blackheath. A number of Romano-British buildings have been found in and around Greenwich, but it's debatable whether the place held much importance for the ruling orders. In fact, once the Romans had faded, the first millennium seems to have passed in more or less total obscurity. Ships spent centuries passing that bend in the river, carrying on up to London or going back out to the sea and then into the Rhine, the great continental waterway leading down the spine of Europe; while nameless Greenwich sat on the shore of the broad Thames, the only hill for miles in that marshy, pre-estuarial flatland.

Eventually it was given a name – either by the Saxon invaders of the sixth and seventh centuries, who called it the 'Green Town'; or by the later, occupying Danes of the ninth century, who called it the 'Green Reach'. Gravesend, by way of contrast, some twenty-five miles downriver, was already a substantial town, where merchant galley ships picked up pilots to lead them upriver, and where the authority of the Saxon port controllers began. At the same time, Merton and Deptford were coming into being as key points on the long stretch into the centre of the city. Still: Greenwich had at least made it as a settlement in its own right, when it appeared in the Domesday Book, produced for William I in 1085–86, as *Grenviz*. From that point on, we can be certain that Greenwich was a place rather than a possibility.

In fact it had already made a small piece of history before the Domesday Book was compiled. In the reign of King Ethelred at the turn of the tenth and eleventh centuries, the marauding Danes had got used to being bought off by the English with a tax – or blackmail, more correctly – known as Danegeld. As part of their campaign of harassment, they seized Aelfheah, Archbishop of Canterbury, in 1011 and held him at Greenwich for seven months, waiting for the payment of a hefty ransom. The money was amassed, but the saintly Aelfheah (or Alphege, as he's now more usually known) refused to let the ransom be paid in his name. So the Danes, in a drunken fury, pelted him to death with the bones from one of their feasts. Immediately he became venerated as a great Christian martyr, and was later interred with due splendour at Canterbury Cathedral, but not before giving his name to the first parish church of Greenwich, built on the site of his martyrdom – now the spot occupied by Hawksmoor's doomy St Alfege's.

After that, though, it's the greenness of Greenwich which becomes its dominating characteristic in comparison with the rest of London, and which shapes its history over the next centuries. The medieval city was starting to grow, and by the fifteenth century London – already the biggest port in the country – was carrying on a huge trade with the rest of the world. Food and wine came in at Billingsgate; timbers, furs, iron and flax from the Baltic came in at Dowgate, just upriver of London Bridge; Queenhithe received grain, salt and iron; Woolwharf, just by Billingsgate, exported wool and cloth. Despite occasional setbacks (the Hundred Years War, for instance), the city grew fat on trade, expanding slowly in all directions, populating the river with ferrymen, lightermen, pilots, fishermen and the captains of trade vessels. The north bank began to fill up with mills, docks, wharves and ships, stretching from the docks at St Katharine's to Wapping, Limehouse and even as far as

Blackwall. This was a major maritime centre, sprawling for miles along the side of the river, and permanently busy with traffic. The business of fishing in the Pool of London became seriously circumscribed, on account of the number of boats and boat-related activities that the Thames had to find room for. Indeed, after 1488 all fishing by net was banned between Wapping Mill and London Bridge. The city was laying down the pattern for everything that followed in later centuries: greater and greater exploitation of land on the north side, greater industrialisation, the constant driving energy of commerce, stronger demands on limited resources.

On the south bank, well below London Bridge, things were a lot quieter. Down at medieval Greenwich, an important religious establishment had been founded, boasting international connections and about to play a key role in the development of the place; but from a commercial point of view, ferrying, fishing and boat maintenance were the main riverside activities. There were some pig farms at Charlton, to the east. Rotherhithe, upriver, was not much more than a small maritime settlement with a pious brotherhood of pilots who prayed for shipwrecked mariners.

What changed things was the arrival of royalty. There were already sightings of monarchs as far back as 1300, when it seems likely that Edward I stayed at Greenwich, making an offering at the chapel of the Virgin Mary; and in 1408, Henry IV dated his will from Greenwich. But the establishment of royalty really got under way in 1417, when the manor of Greenwich passed to Humphrey, Duke of Gloucester, brother of the late Henry V. Duke Humphrey not only enclosed the 200-odd acres of Greenwich Park, but also built a palace for himself by the riverside, which he called Bella Court. After his death, this became the residence of Margaret of Anjou, wife of Henry VI; then the Palace of Placentia ('the pleasant place'), and subsequently central to the lives of Henry VII, Henry VIII, Mary I, Elizabeth I, James I, Charles I and Charles II: an astonishing succession of crowned heads.

It was Henry VII who gave Greenwich its royal lustre. Having taken over Duke Humphrey's palace and rebuilt it on a fittingly regal scale, he made Greenwich a centre of attention in a way in which it had never been before. People started to move down there and build mansions for themselves, to be near the royal court. Merchants and traders were already starting to set up their offices by the fishing port in order to transact their business with the continent; but with the added weight of royalty and its hangers-on, they found themselves caught up in a more dynamic and intriguing environment than commerce alone could have accounted for. And for the next century or so, Placentia remained a focal point of royal life – extensively remodelled by Henry VIII, who adored it, and then much used by Elizabeth I. This gave Greenwich a centrality – despite its location – which powered all the developments we can now see scattered across this corner of south-east London like treasures washed up after a shipwreck. After sixteenth-century Placentia came the seventeenth-century Queen's House, which led indirectly to the Royal Observatory at the end of the same century (which in turn led, ultimately, to the Greenwich Meridian). At the end of the seventeenth and beginning of the eighteenth centuries this was followed by the Royal Naval College (the royals themselves had moved on but still kept up an interest in Greenwich), which prompted the largely Georgian Rangers House, the development of Croom's Hill, the faded Regency prettiness of College Approach – and even the old Woolwich Dockyard, a couple of miles to the east, and the historically charged names in Deptford to the west. If Humphrey, Duke of Gloucester, hadn't taken a liking to the riverside site, then none of this would have happened.

Of course, there is a key historical process at work in Greenwich's history: one of royal infatuation, which grows, blooms and then fades away. And once the monarchy started to lose interest in Greenwich, at some time in the eighteenth century, so the really great building developments gradually came to a halt and the town found itself casting around for another role to play. It had the Observatory and the naval connections, to say nothing of its international prominence among map-makers and seafarers, resulting from the meridian and Greenwich Mean Time. But for the rest of the world – the non-maritime, non-cartographical, land-dwelling world – it was essentially a leisure and tourism spot. The Greenwich Fair (which took place in

Greenwich Park from the mid-eighteenth century onwards) was a key point in the London calendar if you were young, rowdy and in the mood for excitement. Pleasure-boats sailed down the river every day during the summer, regularly disgorging hundreds of sightseers eager to visit the Naval College, walk in the park, check the big exterior clock on the Observatory wall. The fresh fish which were a staple of the very first Greenwich settlers became so popular in the nineteenth century that vast formal dinners of whitebait were eaten – as a tradition – by the government's ministers at the end of each parliamentary session. And despite the gradual encroachments of light industries, wharves, a huge gasworks (at one time the biggest in Europe) on the Greenwich peninsula, and two world wars – that is very much what Greenwich has remained: a tourist locale of unparalleled historical, scientific and architectural interest; a suburb with such an embarrassment of cultural artefacts that even when you know how they all got there, it's sometimes hard to believe that so much is concentrated in one small space.

And so – when we return to the late seventeenth century and the events leading up to the founding of the Royal Naval Hospital, we find that Greenwich still enjoyed that all-important royal favour. It was prominent in the minds of William and Mary: and they had the power to make things happen. A crucial moment arrived in 1692, after the dramatic naval victory of the British over Louis XIV of France at the battle of La Hogue. It was then that Mary II determined to build what she called a hospital – an almshouse for elderly or destitute seamen – on the site of the old Palace of Placentia; which by then was in ruins.

There had already been plans, on and off, for such an institution since Restoration times, when it became clear that it was in no one's interests to have the capital city filling up with the helpless and impoverished ex-mariners who overwhelmed London when discharged *en masse* by the fleet. In 1665 Samuel Pepys – working in the Navy Office, which had been moved to Greenwich from London, on account of the Plague – observed with some despair the after-effects of the Navy's successful encounters with the Dutch. He noted that he 'Did business, though not much at the office, because of the horrible crowd and lamentable moan of the poor seamen, that lie starving in the streets for lack of money, which do trouble and perplex me to the heart; and more at noon, when we were to go through them, for then above a whole hundred of them followed us; some cursing, some swearing and some praying to us.'

It took another thirty years before anything practical was done. In 1694 Sir Christopher Wren was chosen as the architect, initially with a brief to expand on work begun earlier by John Webb for a new royal palace for Charles II at Greenwich. This unfinished palace was the building referred to by Samuel Pepys in his March 1664 diary entry: 'At Greenwich, did observe the foundacion laying of a very great house for the King, which will cost a great deal of money.' But this project had ground to a halt by the end of the decade, as the king's interest dwindled and the finances with it. Wren's task was to incorporate whatever Webb had left behind, and use it as the foundation of a wholly new scheme. Wren had already completed the majority of his great public buildings by this time (St Paul's Cathedral, over fifty London churches, the Royal Hospital at Chelsea, buildings in Oxford and Cambridge, additions to Hampton Court Palace and Kensington Palace), and this was to be the last flowering of his genius. It was the only one of his buildings still to be under construction after the completion of St Paul's in 1711. It was his professional swan-song – and he volunteered his services free of charge: in his words, he dedicated himself to the task in order to 'Have some share in a work of mercy'. Nevertheless, it can't have been far from his mind that, paid or not, he would be able to use Greenwich as an impressive canvas on which to display his talents.

His first drawings were for a great single group of buildings, stretching along the shoreline. However, Queen Mary insisted that he leave the view of the river from the Queen's House unrestricted – even though, when her house was first built, the river view had been blocked by what remained of the old Tudor Placentia. So Wren had to divide his proposed structure into blocks, keeping what Webb had begun on the western side, mirroring it to the east, and then providing a link back to Inigo Jones's building, higher up on the hill, by means of two more separate blocks, closing in towards each other and making the now-familiar parenthesis on either side of the Queen's House. It was a constraint which caused Wren endless dissatisfaction, but about which he could do nothing; and it caused Samuel Johnson to remark, nearly a century later, that the effect was 'Too much detached to make one great whole'. Nevertheless, on 30 June 1696, work officially started. As John Evelyn recorded in his diary: 'I went with a select Committee of the Commissioners for Greenwich Hospital, and with Sir Christopher Wren, where with him I laid the first stone of the intended foundation, precisely at 5 o'clock in the evening, after we had din'd together. Mr Flamstead, the K's astronomical Professor, observing the punctual time by instruments.'

It was quite a collaborative project. Nicholas Hawksmoor worked closely with Wren on much of the design – you can see his hand all over the west front of the King William block – before Sir John Vanbrugh came in to oversee the conclusion of the building programme in the mid-eighteenth century, some thirty years after Wren's death in 1723. Given this amount of egomaniacal genius – and in Wren, Hawksmoor and Vanbrugh you have three of the greatest figures in British architecture – focused on one problem, it's astonishing that the finished building is as coherent as it is, while at the same time so full of expressive touches. A contemporary French commentator, noting that St James's Palace, the principal royal residence in London until the creation of Buckingham Palace, was actually no more than an old leper hospital, revamped by Henry VIII, wrote that 'The kings of England are lodged like invalids at the palace of St. James, and the invalids of the Army and Navy like kings at Chelsea and Greenwich'.

Which returns us to Greenwich now: the long, moody waterfront; the grey, blustery Thames with its odd, solitary boat inching past; the hill in the distance; and the Royal Naval College, empty and under-used, but as fabulous and inexplicable as the royal Palace of Placentia. For several years it's been in a state of transition, being given up by the Royal Navy and the Ministry of Defence, and being taken over partly by the National Maritime Museum, partly by Greenwich University. MoD police have nevertheless been stolidly guarding the west entrance gate all this time, advising visitors not to cross over the low metal chain separating the footpath from the King Charles block and the Grand Square – the plot of lawn leading down to the water's edge, with a 1735 statue of George II in the centre.

So when you visit it, you pass through the west gate and immediately find yourself in another world – a world of classically inspired rustication, stone pilasters, pediments, Corinthian capitals, the world Wren created when the Royal Naval College was in its first incarnation, as the Royal Naval Hospital. The very first building on your right is a red herring, an addition to the Wren/Hawksmoor plan by another hand entirely. This is the old Dreadnought Seamen's Hospital, built in 1764 by James

'Athenian' Stuart (the architect who brought back the highly influential three-volume work *The Antiquities of Athens* from his tour of the classical world; and who later redesigned the interior of the Royal Naval Hospital Chapel), and is not a true original, any more than the old stable block and the Victorian Pepys Building opposite are originals. You have to make your way between these two, before the Naval Hospital spreads out triumphantly before you – with on your left, the King Charles block, started in 1664 by John Webb; and on your right, the King William block, a Wren and Hawksmoor joint effort, dating from 1698. Two things may strike you. The first is that here you have three architects – one of whom had no contact with the other two – conspiring to make a brilliantly unified (but not unvarying) whole, rather than a jigsaw of mismatches. And the second thing is that the scale and look of the place are monumental to the point of being positively unfriendly. Wren's classicism was always empirical enough not to be overly strict – subsequent generations of architects would criticise his work for its lack of classical rigidity – but with its colonnades and domes and repetitions, there's a coldness in the place, a formality which makes you feel awkward. It may just be a question of the temperament of the time in which it was built failing to match the temperament of the age that looks upon it; or it may be something darkly un-English about the whole edifice. The waterfront face – the eastern, or Queen Anne block, being more or less a copy of Webb's western precursor – is classically grand, but with a slight Inigo Jones-ish restraint about it. Webb was, after all, Jones's pupil and his apologist after Jones's death. But the more Wren takes charge, the more daunting it gets – culminating in the landmark baroque domes on the King William and Queen Mary blocks.

But then, this is something which also happens with Wren's triumphant St Paul's Cathedral. Astonishing as St Paul's is, it also has a cold authority, moated by Cannon Street to the south and the empty plaza of Paternoster Square to the north. Looming massively over all the buildings nearby, it awes them into silence – especially Paternoster's 1960s modernism, now completely lifeless and dumbstruck. Here are the workings of Wren's mind, made real, in Portland stone and marble, and they do remind you that he was a professor of astronomy and a brilliant mathematician, as well as being the most famous of all British architects. As with St Paul's, so with the Royal Naval Hospital – even though temperamentally such a building ought to be closer to his Royal Hospital at Chelsea, with its lawns, its warmer brickwork, its friendlier dimensions, than to one of the biggest churches in the country. There seems to be a disjunction between the purpose of the building and its appearance – too much triumphalism over Louis XIV, not enough creature comforts.

This continues in the hands of Wren's protégé, Hawksmoor. Those strange, sweeping curves at the tops of the end pavilions of the west front of the King William block, which Hawksmoor completed in 1708; those daunting columns and pilasters, the massive stonework forms and the strangely truncated and ornamented linking sections, two-thirds the height of the rest of the composition, all conspire to impress you with Hawksmoor's genius; and to make you wish that it wasn't quite so challenging, quite so individualistic. (Nor are they helped by the air of necromancy which has hung over Hawksmoor's name ever since Peter Ackroyd's startling mixture of detective story and historical fantasy, *Hawksmoor*.) As a consequence – and no matter how unjust or irrational the feeling may be – it's hard to look on one of his buildings now and not feel uncomfortable. Even his church of St Alfege's, in the nearby High Road, is a bit of a frightener. Built in 1714, it was designed to replace the old parish church of St Alfege's, where Thomas Tallis had once been royal organist and which had fallen down in the great storm of 1710. But instead of a parish church, Greenwich got a small cathedral, with huge columns and pilasters on the east portico (expressive of the aptly named colossal order of which Hawksmoor and Vanbrugh were so fond) and collections of weird, heavily stylised urns ornamenting the roofline. The effect is powerful, even minatory – not just because of the cramped surroundings of central Greenwich which it effectively dwarfs with its huge presence, but because the building is also normally locked and dark, adding an extra note of menace. It makes you wonder quite what Hawksmoor had in mind when he drew up the plans.

*

But there's another dimension to the Naval Hospital, beyond Wren's magnificence and Hawksmoor's strangeness. While much of the Royal Naval Hospital is off-limits, you can still look at two of the most extraordinary rooms in London, both built for the hospital's pensioners, both as daunting as Wren's exterior, both using quite different techniques to impress.

The earlier of the two is the Painted Hall, situated in the King William block. Hawksmoor was responsible for the design, around 1704, but Sir James Thornhill painted the interior in a fantastical baroque style, between 1708 and 1727. Thornhill was in fact the pre-eminent historical painter of the day, and not only completed the interior of the Painted Hall, but also did the eight scenes in the dome of St Paul's Cathedral, as well as paintings at Blenheim and Hampton Court. You can actually see him depicted in the Upper Hall, a figure at ground level on the right-hand side of the painting of Queen Anne and Prince George with the Virtues. His artist's palette is shelved on a *trompe-l'oeil* pillar behind him and while his right hand gestures towards the monarch, his left seems to be scrounging a tip. He was paid £6,685 2s. 4d. for his work – £3 a square yard for the ceilings and £1 a yard for the walls: not a huge sum for nineteen years' work, even for the first half of the eighteenth century and, by all accounts, a bill reluctantly met. Given the hint of a backhander in his pose, plus his jaded expression, he may well have seen himself as something of the put-upon artist, at the mercy of his employers' whims.

Nevertheless, he and his assistants managed to complete a staggering piece of sheer theatrical decoration. On the vast ceiling of the Lower Hall, Peace and Liberty triumph over Tyranny, in the form of William and Mary crushing a scurvy-looking Louis XIV. Apollo dashes across the heavens in the chariot of the sun, the signs of the zodiac peep over the oval frame; while fire, earth, air and water are all involved, to say nothing of Truth, Time, the Four Seasons, Architecture, British rivers, the spoils of war, fighting ships, plus ranks of *trompe-l'oeil* pilasters marching down the walls towards grisaille fake weapons and instruments at the end. In the Upper Hall – where in later years the officer classes would eat – an immense confection involving Queen Anne and her husband, Prince George of Denmark, rears up in a billowing mass of semi-nude classical figures, wings, fruits, clouds – with St Paul's Cathedral bulking up behind. IAM NOVA PROGENIES CŒLO says the motto above this colossal frieze: NOW A NEW RACE FROM HEAVEN. Three huge refectory tables in the Lower Hall, each around 35 yards long, can seat some 240 diners, comfortably lit by files of silver candelabra. These alone would be impressive enough; but they add a sense of scale and perspective to the room, making Thornhill's work look even bigger, grander, more awe-inspiring.

As, in its way, is the interior of the Chapel of St Peter and St Paul, completed by James Stuart in 1789. Originally, the chapel was to a design by Wren, completed after his death by Thomas Ripley in 1752. But in 1779 the whole interior was destroyed by a fire (which started in a tailor's shop in the rooms below), and

Stuart was drafted in to create a new chapel in a style reflecting the changing tastes of the late eighteenth century. Where the hall is vast, billowing and baroque, the chapel is big, bright, neo-classical and in its way even more of a vision. Unlike the hall, the only canvas of any size here is a large altarpiece by Benjamin West, PRA. This depicts St Paul being preserved from the ship-wreck on Malta and grappling with the viper that came out of the fire: 'And he shook off the beast into the fire, and felt no harm' (Acts 28:5). While this is big, imposing and sombre – and, dealing with the apostle's delivery from a storm at sea, highly apt for a congregation of mariners – it's nowhere near as imposing as Thornhill's decorative work in the Painted Hall. What is aston-ishing, though, is the plasterwork which covers the walls and the ceiling: repeated shapes of shells, leaves, swags, vases, cherubs, dolphins, octagons, interlocking key motifs, lozenges, wings, wreaths – the whole sourcebook thrown at anything flat enough to take a moulding. The architectural critic Ian Nairn once wrote that 'It has an impersonal and rather chilling sense of power that does not feel English at all; perhaps it might be more at home in Lenigrad', and you can see what he meant – the ruthlessness, the scale, the machine-like precision of the design, combined with the chocolate-box colouring (duck egg blue, shades of beige, pink grace notes) are both severely regimented and weirdly profligate, dramatic but crushing. One of the philosophical premises behind the neoclassical revival from the mid-eighteenth to the early nineteenth century, was that the decorative excesses of baroque and rococo design should be expunged, and replaced by a greater simplicity and classical truthfulness. Somehow this precept seems to have been lost in 'Athenian' Stuart's positively obsessive treatment of St Peter and St Paul.

Like almost everything else in the Naval Hospital, this awe-inspiring display of talents – which would look fine in a royal palace, or some institution deliberately designed to cow its visitors (the Foreign Office of the nineteenth century, perhaps; the headquarters of the Bank of England) – hardly seems right for a place where humble seamen were supposed to spend the twilight of their lives.

So is it surprising to learn that the Greenwich Hospital eventually failed, and was given up as an almshouse in 1869, becoming the Naval College four years later?

Certainly, the Naval Hospital had started well enough. Its 1694 Charter of Foundation, stated that the first object of the place was to be 'The relief and support of seamen aboard the ships and vessels belonging to the Royal Navy . . . who by reason of age, wound or other disabilities shall be incapable of further service at sea and be unable to maintain themselves . . .' What's more, it was endowed with enough money to keep it staffed and in good repair, and to pay a small weekly stipend to the 3,000 pensioners for whom it was designed. The endowment money came from several sources, including the Crown itself, private donors, the sixpence a month deducted from seamen's pay, a tax on coal, smuggling fines, captured pirates' treasure and a national lottery (which, oddly enough, enjoyed little success). It was, in other words, properly funded, properly organised, and even enjoyed the luxury of its own brewery and bakery on site. Admissions took place every fortnight, at which time new entrants had to give up whatever pensions they were currently receiving, leave their wives behind (a particularly cruel requirement, and one which may well have contributed to the institution's demise), be washed, disinfected and shaved, and then fitted into the hospital's uniform of a dark blue coat, sleeved waistcoat, breeches and cocked hat. The weekly allowance (known as 'tobacco money') started at one shilling, gradually rising over the decades to five shillings. Pensioners could also make a bit extra by showing visitors around the buildings (especially Thornhill's Painted Hall), caddying for golfers on Blackheath and renting out telescopes in Greenwich Park. This last was a guaranteed way to make money, as visitors were morbidly keen to train their spyglasses on the shoreline of the Thames, where the bloated corpses of condemned criminals could be seen, bobbing up and down on the tide – having been chained up and drowned there. In 1764 the hospital governor, Admiral Lord Rodney, optimistically declared – one hundred years after the laying of the foundation stone – that 'It shall be the rule of my conduct to render the old men's lives so comfortable that the younger shall say when he goes away, "Who would not be a sailor to live as happy as a prince in his old age!"'

But there was something wrong. Only seven years after Lord Rodney's proud declamation, one Captain Baillie was drawing attention to the fact that the pensioners – no matter how grand their surroundings – were expected to sleep in cabins no more than seven feet square; that 'The privies were a perpetual source of offensive odours'; that the 'veal was in the highest degree disgusting and the beer tended to give convulsive gripes, being thick, sour and odorous'; and the 'columns, colonnades and friezes ill accord with bully beef and sour beer mixed with water'. Nathaniel Hawthorne – who lived in Blackheath for a short period in the mid-nineteenth century – also picked up this imbalance between style and charity: 'Pillars and porticos produce but a cold and shivering effect in the English climate. I would have studied the characters, habits and predilections of nautical people . . . and would have built in the hospital a kind of ethereal simulate to the narrow, dark, ugly and inconvenient, but snug and cosy homeliness of the sailor boarding-houses.' In 1845, Sir John Liddell, director-general of the Medical Department of the Royal Navy and inspector-general of the Royal Hospital, added his voice to the growing litany of complaints, paying particular attention to the fact that Greenwich was no longer the grassy bucolic riverside retreat it had been for the Tudors, but had been sucked into the maw of London, which was growing with all the ugly vitality that the nineteenth century could muster. He railed against 'The inconveniences and nuisances to which it' – the Hospital – 'is exposed from the daily increase of houses and manufactories that hem it in on all sides, which necessarily impede the external ventilation and subject the inmates to the injurious influence of air vitiated by the clouds of dense black smoke and impurities that are being driven upon it from the chimney tops of steamers and manufactories that are gathering around it'.

But even that wasn't all. There were by now constant accusations of cruelty and maladministration, of ill-treatment of pensioners by high-handed and callous governors, of bullying and hostility between the former ranks. An atmosphere of rancour and maltreatment prevailed. According to a report of 1860, 'Quarrelling, fighting, drunkenness and personal filthiness convert some wards into absolute pandemonium'. The worst of it was probably the sheer boredom of long hours in restricted circumstances, with nothing to do but nurture old grudges. The same report admitted as much, confessing that 'Debauchery is their only resource against ennui'. Eventually the number of pensioners dwindled, in a fog of disillusion and resentment, and the establishment was wound down in the 1860s. Too grand, too awkward, too cold, too intimidating, too unfriendly for the pensioners it housed, it turned out to be an architectural masterpiece which failed the purpose for which it was built. At the Chelsea Hospital, the Chelsea Pensioners are still there in their red Duke of Marlborough uniforms, and have been there since the institution opened in 1692. At Greenwich, they lasted a hundred and fifty years and then gave up.

*

But by 1873, Wren's design had been given a second chance: the government had decided to establish the new Royal Naval College in his buildings. This college was actually an amalgamation of two existing institutions – the Naval College at Portsmouth and the School of Naval Architecture and Marine Engineering, based in Kensington. The idea was to give the Royal Navy the kind of highly trained and skilled officers it was going to need in the technologically advanced new world of steam power and complex armaments that confronted Britain at the end of the nineteenth century. The first admiral president of the college, Vice-Admiral Sir Astley Cooper Key – something of a scholar (and by Navy standards, an Einstein) – chose as college motto, TAM MINERVA QUAM MARTE – by wisdom as much as by war. The general aim of the new outfit was, 'By cultivating the general intelligence of officers, to improve their aptitude for the various duties which a naval officer is called upon to perform'. Subjects included naval history and architecture, mechanical and electrical engineering, chemistry, navigation, and a tremendous amount of mathematics.

All of this deeply irritated die-hard naval conservatives, who reckoned that common sense, orderliness and a degree of seamanship (which could only be taught on board a ship, in the old way) were all that a commanding officer needed, and that an understanding of hydrodynamics was totally beyond the point. As a result of this (and the fact that young officers who had been at sea for some years before finding themselves in the relaxed

landlocked atmosphere of Greenwich, frequently went mad with
drink and depravity) it took years for the Royal Naval College to
establish a name for itself. Even Admiral Fisher, First Sea Lord
and promoter of all kinds of improvements and modernisations
in the Navy (including the Dreadnought battleship), hated the
college – partly because he disliked its emphasis on academic
attainment; partly because he detested Greenwich itself. 'Of all
the places in the United Kingdom,' he wrote, at the start of the
twentieth century, 'Greenwich is the most unsuitable . . . During
the winter it is damp and almost continually enveloped in fog
and mist . . . The surroundings of the College are practically one
huge slum!' Instead of giving his men plenty of fresh air and
exercise, the college kept them trapped in overheated studies
surrounded by wet fog, as a consequence of which most student
officers came down with debilitating bronchial infections.

But at least it grew into its role – that of a true naval university – over the years, expanding and consolidating, and becoming
a recognised part of the Navy's structure. Wren's buildings suited
it perfectly. It was dignified, historical, spacious and entirely
appropriate for the Senior Service. Not only could it fit in living
accommodation, lecture rooms and a library, it even had room
for a small experimental nuclear reactor. Which is why it seemed
unduly cruel for the Ministry of Defence to decide, in the mid-
1990s, that as the Navy itself was shrinking, so were its
educational needs; and that the staff colleges of the Army, Navy
and Air Force should be merged into one – for the time being

located in the Air Force College at Cranwell, in Lincolnshire. A real reflection of changing priorities, from sea to air. So the University of Greenwich took on one part of the old college; the National Maritime Museum took on another. And the rest sits and waits.

There's something about the fantastical palace of Greenwich Hospital which has left it permanently unsettled, as it shifts from almshouse to Royal Naval College to university annexe and museum extension, without ever seeming to fix on one use, without ever seeming to know for certain why it's there. The builders and restorers move in, the tarpaulins and dust sheets go up, contractors' vans litter the margins: another attempt to settle the hospital's destiny. Instead of feeling sweeping confidence – something derived from the audacity and self-belief that must have driven Wren and Hawksmoor – you experience a sensation of being left behind in the race, as if it's only a matter of time before the fate which has overtaken Trafalgar Quarters will slowly overtake the Naval College – Trafalgar Quarters being the handsome two-storeyed building next door, dating from 1813, once lodgings for officers at the hospital, a charming model of dignity and classical rightness with its stonework, its arcades and its colonnade – and now closed up, chained and padlocked, with weeds growing out of the drive.

But there they are, these magnificent buildings, marooned out in SE10, on a bend of the river, in fabulous isolation, with the Docklands Light Railway and Canary Wharf on the far bank, the tide lapping the steps of Five Foot Walk, the old royal landing place just in front of the wonderful 1849 River Gate. And they're there principally because at one time Greenwich was very dear to the hearts of the kings and queens of England.

ROYAL

THE PRESENCE of royalty made Greenwich. But it took some time for the effect to become apparent. In fact, you have to go back to the 900s to see where royal Greenwich comes from. Up to this point, apart from some interest from the Romans, there was very little happening on this stretch of the river. But before his death in 899, King Alfred settled the place he called Gronovic (the Anglo-Saxon Greenwich) on his youngest daughter, Elstrudis, supposedly as a dowry on her marriage to Baldwin II, Count of Flanders, one of the most influential men in Europe. When Baldwin died, in 918, Elstrudis gave the manor of Greenwich (as well as Lewisham and Woolwich) to the abbey at Ghent as a memorial to her late husband. Thus begins an association between Flanders and England, which carried on for the next few centuries and which helped to concentrate attention on this area near London.

So far as the Abbey of Ghent was concerned, Greenwich was useful as a source of cash revenue. There were rents to collect on properties in the manor, and an assortment of other dues, tolls and tithes related to aspects of life in Greenwich. There was also a building, or collection of buildings down by the river, known as Old Court, standing on the spot now occupied by the Royal Naval College. This substantial holding would have been run at arm's length by the Abbot of Ghent, as a hostel for visiting priors and abbots of other ecclesiastical institutions, and as a place in which he could hold his own courts in style. Of course, this created local friction. There was resentment at a foreign institution creaming off levies and rents from an English neighbourhood, no matter how legitimate the set-up. There was nervousness about the presence of potentially hostile foreigners in large numbers at a militarily significant bend in the River Thames. There were complaints that the Abbot was failing to carry out the religious duties imposed on him by the conditions of Elstrudis's gift. As the years went by, the manor became more and more of a burden, and less and less of a benefit. And so the hapless Abbot of Ghent gradually allowed the manor to fall away, bit by bit, until Henry V finally disallowed the possessions of alien monasteries in 1414, and the Old Court at Greenwich became the property of the Crown.

But Greenwich was still of interest, without being the centre of attention. It was not, yet, a place where huge sums of money would go towards building some of the most extravagant pieces of architecture in the country.

It took the arrival of Humphrey, Duke of Gloucester, to make Greenwich special. The fourth son of Henry IV, Humphrey had been acting regent for the infant king, Henry VI (born in 1421) after the death of Henry V in 1422; a job he gradually lost to his rival, Cardinal Henry Beaufort, the half-brother of Henry IV. Soldier, politician and schemer, the Duke of Gloucester was more generally known as 'Good Duke Humphrey', on account of his promotion of humanism in England and his generous passion for learning. By the mid-1420s he was hoping to establish himself with a degree of elegance in a place where he could collect works of literature and increase the sum of human knowledge. Greenwich struck him as the right place, and once he had cleared questions of legal title, he started building after 1426.

His palace was Bella Court, and the 200 acres of neighbouring land he was later allowed to enclose (including 'pasture, wood, heath, furze and gorse') ultimately became Greenwich Park. Bella Court itself may have been one of the finest houses in fifteenth-century England: Duke Humphrey was given permission to put up 'A mansion, crenelled and embattled, and enclose it within walls, also to erect and turrelate a certain tower, all in stone and lime'. Having done so, he then crammed it with fine possessions – embroidery, jewels, silverware – and an enormous quantity of books. This was the first great library in England to be owned by a private individual rather than an ecclesiastical institution. He used an agent called Candido to search Europe for interesting and important works, filling his shelves with the writings of Plato, Livy, Cicero, Dante and Petrarch, as well as commissioning works from the English poet John Lydgate and the chronicler John Capgrave. The latter, naturally enough, referred to Duke Humphrey as 'The most lettered prince in the world'. It was a prodigious collection, and it was mostly intended – a truly splendid gesture – to form the nucleus of the library at Oxford University; which until then had been relatively starved of books and, consequently, of learning. Not only did Duke Humphrey leave this priceless collection as a single library for the university after his death (the library subsequently becoming the Bodleian, after Sir Thomas Bodley restored it in 1602), but he also had a reading room built for it, which is still known as Duke Humphrey's Library.

But while the library in Oxford is still there, none of Bella Court is. Frustratingly for us, the only bits that see the light of day come up on archaeological digs or during reconstruction work. Bits of the Flemish Old Court also emerge from time to time, but Old Court and Bella Court are now so deeply buried in the foundations of later buildings that it's impossible to gain much of a sense of what they were like. All we can do is speculate that Bella Court was rich, red brick, imposing, much of the time filled with visiting writers, politicians and intellectuals. And this would have been one of the causes of the Good Duke's downfall. One historian claims that 'The house by the Thames must have seemed, to Englishmen at any rate, the centre of the civilised world' – too much of a cynosure, in fact, to the country's rulers in those unstable and treacherous times. After the psychologically troubled and ineffectual Henry VI effectively assumed the throne in 1437, decades of squabbling and betrayal followed, as part of which Humphrey, Duke of Gloucester was summoned to Bury St Edmunds in February 1447, arrested and found mysteriously dead in his cell the next day: a political force neutralised.

So what happened to Bella Court? It was promptly appropriated by Henry VI's scheming wife, Margaret of Anjou, who already coveted the riverside palace. The first thing she did was change the name from Bella Court to the Frenchified Plesaunce. She spent a small fortune putting in terracotta tiles bearing her monogram, filling the windows with costly new glass patterned with daisies, building a landing-stage, a treasure house, courts and pavilions, lengths of pavement, bay windows, and luxurious new personal apartments. Her own bedchamber was paved with Flanders tiles, had a door ornamented with 200 tin nails, and a state bed costing 8s. 6d., delivered from London. This by all accounts ruthlessly ambitious woman spent the best part of five years prettifying Duke Humphrey's house, turning it into a place of pink brick, white stone and multitudinous detail. The royal dynamic had arrived, conspicuously.

Greenwich was, by then, starting to acquire some weight.

Already it had an established market, as well as an important anchorage for boats travelling to and from the continent, plus boat sheds, wharves and all kinds of marine businesses – and enough citizens of wealth and rank to make the place seem important. Some may have come to be part of Duke Humphrey's court; others arrived when Margaret of Anjou settled there. It was no longer just a bend in the river with fishermen, ferrymen and a very big house on the water's edge.

But Plesaunce itself was doomed. As the Wars of the Roses dragged on, Margaret of Anjou vanished; then the next occupant, the controversial Elizabeth Woodville, wife of Edward IV, was forcibly retired to nearby Bermondsey Abbey. Henry VII took charge of Plesaunce at the end of the fifteenth century and immediately had it razed to the ground. That would have been that for the site of Old Court, Bella Court and Plesaunce, but for the fact that the king at once started to build a bigger, more modern palace on the same spot, creating one of the principal royal residences of the day. He called it Placentia, the pleasant place, a Latin variant on Margaret of Anjou's Plesaunce. Placentia, it would seem, was nearly as big as Hampton Court (which dates principally from 1514) and built of a similar grand mixture of masses of red brick with formal white stone dressings.

Henry VII also had the Palace of Sheen, in Richmond, Surrey, to enjoy – to say nothing of the castle at Windsor, established by William I and much enlarged by Henry II and Henry III – a proper fortress, capable of withstanding heavy attack. No sooner had he finished work on Placentia than he began refurbishment of the palace at Richmond (damaged by fire), so that by around 1510 he had two splendid riverside seats, with Windsor as a third option. Richmond is in some ways a mirror of Greenwich: close enough to London to constitute a part of it, easy to get to by boat; but far enough away to escape the fumes and distempers of the city and the Palace of Westminster. As in Greenwich, there was also a vantage point – Richmond Hill – rising up from the water's edge to provide dramatic topographical contrast, with fine views and the freshest airs. Of course, Greenwich had not only salty estuarial breezes (unlike Richmond's stuffier inland climate), it also had good fresh water and drainage, plus the opportunity to watch the river traffic bringing precious goods and sweetmeats into London – something Henry VIII also loved to do in later years. Which was Henry VII's favourite? Probably Richmond; but Greenwich must have come a very close second.

Certainly, Placentia was a big enough establishment once the building works were over. The state and royal rooms were at the river front, while countless apartments and chambers grouped themselves around a network of courtyards. Judging by an engraving made by James Basire in 1767 from a much earlier painting, Placentia presented a long, low face to the river, mostly no more than two storeys tall, punctuated with towers, crested by a line of castellations and with a single massive gateway – or *donjon* – at the eastern end. Somewhere behind this, the warren of smaller rooms and buildings would have begun, among the chimneys and steeply pitched roofs.

The Wars of Roses had ended in 1485, so Henry could enjoy himself in Greenwich as much as his repressive nature would allow. Once or twice, admittedly, the aftermath of the wars would disturb him, in the form of Lambert Simnel or Perkin Warbeck; while in 1497 he had to put down a mass of rebellious Cornishmen who had collected on Blackheath. But otherwise, Placentia was turned over to after-the-fighting celebrations. Jousting, feasting, parades, music, whoring and indulgence of all kinds took place. The presence of the court meant that the number of great houses in the area multiplied: soon there was a large establishment known as Copped Hall; there was the house of the king's chamberlain, the Earl of Worcester; there was Sir William Compton's house; and a building known as the great Swanne House. In 1491 the future Henry VIII was born at Placentia. And with his birth, Greenwich hit a goldmine.

Henry loved Placentia; and what Placentia saw was the young king in the absolute prime of his years, a long way from the bloated paranoiac he became in the 1540s. This was the near-mythical Henry VIII who loved scholarship, who delighted in music, who spent endless hours on horseback, hunting, jousting, issuing challenges – the unstoppable Henry VIII who, uniquely for a Tudor monarch, grew up in the quiet certainty of ascending the throne, and who in his confidence epitomised the brilliant self-belief which England vitally needed at the time. An Italian diplomat, Agostino Guistiniani, writing in 1515, clearly caught the prevailing mood when he described the king as 'Extremely handsome . . . much handsomer than any other sovereign in Christendom . . . He is extremely fond of tennis, at which game it is the prettiest thing in the world to see him play, his fair skin glowing through a shirt of the finest texture.'

As a consequence of Henry's energetic ebullience, Placentia – Greenwich Palace – enjoyed years of revells; and there are many examples of his high spirits and his prodigious liberality. In 1511, for instance, Henry opened up the king's Christmas feast to 'all respectable comers' and then, along with eleven others, dressed up to take part in a fantastical entertainment, 'A thing not seen before,' according to the chronicler Holinshed. For this he had a castle called 'Le Fortresse Dangerus' built in the great hall. In red satin and cloth of gold, Henry – along with five male companions – play-acted an assault on the mock fortress, in which six ladies had been placed in hiding. The king and his friends conquered the castle and brought the ladies out to dance before the queen, Catherine of Aragon – who, it is said, was delighted.

In 1512, Henry held a three-day joust in the palace's tiltyard. Unsurprisingly, he won again, breaking more staves than his nearest rival, the Earl of Essex. In 1514 he staged another mock-attack on a pretend castle, this time with the players clad in blue velvet and cloth of silver. In 1515 he threw a vast public celebration to commemorate the marriage of his sister, Mary, and the next year he did the same again when his other sister, Margaret, came to visit Greenwich. This time the king, the Duke of Suffolk, the Earl of Essex and the Master of the Horse, Nicholas Carew, Esquire, took on all comers in two days of jousting, for which 'Their apparel, and that of their horses, was black-velvet, covered over with branches of honeysuckles of fine flat gold of damask'. For Christmas that year, he commanded an artificial garden to be laid in the great hall, in which the ladies and gentlemen of the court proceeded to dance. In 1518 the French ambassador arrived at Greenwich by barge, to arrange a marriage between the king's two-year-old daughter, Mary, and the Dauphin. For a momentous state occasion such as this, Henry put on a tableau to end all tableaux, incorporating, among other things, a rock on top of which sat a lady with a dolphin in her lap, surrounded by five trees bearing the arms of Rome, the Emperor, England, France and Spain. Out of the rock emerged a group of knights who took part in a tournament, while a man mounted on Pegasus came out to deliver a commentary on the action. After that, a vast banquet was consumed, the food being served on gold plates.

When ambassadors arrived from Scotland at Christmastime in 1522, Henry commanded that a castle be built in the tiltyard. Twenty feet square by fifty feet high, this was made of immense wooden beams held together with iron clasps. It served as a setting for the usual mock-heroics, enacted before the wondering gaze of the ambassadors. Two 'ancient knights' then presented themselves to the queen, and said that 'Though youth had left them, they still had courage, and would like to break spear, if the Queen would give them leave'. Catherine consented, the old men threw off their disguises and revealed themselves as none other than the king and the Duke of Suffolk. The Scots ambassadors found all this enormously diverting, and asked 'whether the King was as merry during war as during peace, and, on being answered in the affirmative, said they were surprised at that, for the Scotch mourned and wailed in war time'.

And if this wasn't enough, the month of May in every year – special visitors or no – ushered in a whole season of sporting competitions: archery, combat with spears and battleaxes, wrestling, and casting the light and heavy bars. Each day's sport would end with the queen giving out the prizes (the first, naturally, to the king who, being six feet tall, powerfully built, overwhelmingly energetic and the monarch, tended to win) and with the herald's cry, 'My Lords, for your noble feats in arms, God give you the love of the ladies you most desire'.

The amount of rebuilding and expansion of the royal palace that all this required was immense. The palace Henry had inherited from his father was already big, but he added to it prodigiously in the early years of his reign. Among his main achievements was to build at Greenwich one of the greatest armouries in the world – a workshop staffed by German and Italian craftsmen, which became famous for 'Suits of mail as deftly joined as a lobster's shell, dispersed and damascened with sweet devices, and richly inlaid with gold'. He also had constructed a banqueting hall designed by William Vertue (the king's master mason) and a – literally – king-sized tiltyard in which to tilt and joust. This was so big that it extended almost to the front of where the Queen's House now stands. There was also a 'Highest Library' in the tower overlooking the river, in which the king kept his impressive book collection; and three principal courtyards – Main, Middle, to the east, and Chapel, to the north of that, with the great hall standing between the Middle and Chapel courtyards. Just outside the main complex of buildings, Henry's deer in Greenwich Park provided game for the royal hunts. The little castle on top of Greenwich Hill – originally put up by Duke Humphrey in the mid-fifteenth century – was rebuilt in 1526, both as a place for the younger members of Henry's family to stay; and as somewhere to keep his mistresses.

The establishment was large; and so were the numbers of people needed to service what was, effectively, a small town. On a normal day there would have been, in attendance on the king, squires, gentlemen, grooms, pages, servers, heralds, messengers, and seven minstrels plus their 'marshal'. Twenty barge rowers were also on the palace staff. In between the duties of state and the overseeing of his more formal entertainments, the king would sweep up part of this retinue and go hawking and hunting in the park: as Guistiniani observed, he was 'very fond of hunting, and never takes his diversion without tiring eight or ten horses –

before he gets home they are all exhausted'. Failing that, he would sit on the roof leads and watch the great vessels of trade carrying silk, gold and spices upriver to London. If gazing at these vessels palled, he could go out and inspect his warships lying at anchor nearby.

Deptford and Woolwich grew fat on Henry's presence at Greenwich. In 1513 he created the Royal Naval Dockyard – otherwise simply known as the King's Yard – in neighbouring Deptford, for the building and maintenance of the fleet of ships which was to become the core of the Royal Navy. His daughter, Elizabeth I, expanded Henry's efforts into Britain's principal defence and the means by which the Empire spread itself around the world; but Henry took the first vital steps. So Deptford was transformed from a fishing village into one of the powerhouses of the new world force; while at the same time, another royal dockyard went up at Woolwich, downriver of Greenwich. This was, in the first instance, a place to build the vast flagship *Great Harry* – also called *Henry Grace a Dieu*. Weighing 1,500 tons, it was easily the largest warship of its day and carried a huge complement of 186 guns. The king had it formally dedicated by the Archbishop of Canterbury (and half the bishops in England) in 1514, in a ceremony in which the prelates 'processed around the ship as she lay in dock, chanting Pater, Ave and Credo, and formally blessing and sprinkling with holy water the hull' (which didn't, however, stop it from meeting a humiliating end in 1553 when, ironically, it burned down at Woolwich, the place which had brought it into being). Undeterred, Woolwich expanded rapidly into the other half of the great military duopoly on this section of the river. And so Henry stamped his presence on Placentia, Greenwich and the whole surrounding area.

The frustrating thing is that there's nothing left to see of it. What can it have been like, in the first decades of the sixteenth century, this centrepiece of Henry's life and ambitions, the palace he loved most? You can get something of the feel of the buildings from those fragments of Richmond Palace which still remain in south-west London. You can admire the looming gateway on Richmond Green bearing the arms of Henry VII, the Old Palace Yard behind – big enough to breathe in, but not so big as to be intimidating – and the restored buildings of the Wardrobe, running down at right angles from the gateway. The brickwork here is dark and busy with that typically Tudor intricacy which looks either oppressive or delightfully old-fashioned – the antithesis of the smooth ashlar of later centuries. The proportions are comfortable and the windows have a cottagey casement aspect which makes the place seem more accommodating than you'd expect of a royal palace.

But the remains at Richmond suggest only part of the picture. A closer comparison might be with Hampton Court Palace, a few miles up the Thames. This came into Henry VIII's hands when its owner, Cardinal Wolsey, handed it over to the king in a futile attempt to get back into his favour. It didn't work for Wolsey (impeachment and arrest, followed by death, were his rewards), but Henry was nonetheless intoxicated with the place, with its 280 guest rooms and its staff of 500. At once he moved in and began a programme of enlargement and embellishment.

Now, if Greenwich Palace was even slightly like Hampton Court – the Tudor Hampton Court, of course, excluding subsequent additions; the Hampton Court very largely created by Wolsey in the period 1514–28, just a little later than Henry's alterations to Greenwich – then it must have been truly magnificent. Hampton's main entrance, the west front, with Base Court behind it, the first and biggest courtyard of the whole complex, is still impressive and romantic. Its turrets, castellations, forests of ornamented chimneys, spirelets and details of stone picked out against the red brickwork have an almost oriental elaborateness, a kind of exoticism. Back in the 1500s, when a building like this would not only have seemed impossibly ornate but also impossibly big, it must have been an awe-inspiring experience to approach it from the river, coming up from below and seeing the great palace rise above you. Inside, were endless carvings, mouldings, painted details, the ceilings frantic with decoration, pendant vaults, gilding; while the walls were covered in tapestries which were both profligate in their designs and of a material richness and quality that startles even today, when they are faded and thinned by the passage of time.

Hampton Court, of course, is above London, where the Thames is narrow and where none of the commercial and naval craft of the lower Thames could reach. It's sleepier – prettier, maybe, but short of the drama that the situation at Greenwich could provide. After all, from the top of Greenwich Hill you can still imagine the view that Henry would have seen: the same unique double reach of the river, endless flatness stretching away on the north bank, the play of light as the sun catches it from the west, the whole scene apparently laid out before you for your own private satisfaction. And if you then imagine on the steely expanse of water an assortment of huge, high-masted ships, each one expressing your own wealth and power and watch *them* as they ply up and down, with your rose-red palace. An abbreviated Hampton Court Palace at the water's edge, it's just possible to get some idea why Henry loved the place so much and why he chose to live in Greenwich rather than, say, the Palace of Westminster, with its marshes, crowds of seedy politicians and other low-lifers, its constant bouts of plague and its city atmosphere.

When the Holy Roman Emperor Charles V paid a visit to his aunt, Catherine of Aragon, and her husband, King Henry, in 1522 – the same year as the startled Scottish ambassadors – he was put in the king's own lodging, which was so richly and profusely decorated that his Spanish attendants 'wondered at it, and especially the rich cloth of estate'. The Holy Roman Emperor was no pauper himself. He arrived with a retinue of 2,000 men and 1,000 horses, necessitating a progress of thirty barges to take himself and his company from Gravesend to Greenwich – a progress for which all the ships in the Thames were arranged in lines, adorned with streamers, and ordered to fire off round after round of salutes. Once the Emperor was installed, more fierce entertainments followed. Lances were broken in jousting, while a huge banqueting house was specially put up for the occasion in the tiltyard and furnished with amusing and fantastical decoration – dragons, lions, a gilded and painted mock ceiling, a fountain, greyhounds . . .

But even that wasn't the pinnacle of Henry's achievements as a host. After the failure (as it turned out) of Charles V's betrothal to Mary, the French and English tried again in 1527, this time to pair Mary off with the recently widowed Francis I of France. Among others, Gabriel de Grammont, Antoine de Viste – President of Paris and Brittany – and François, Vicomte de Turrenne, all arrived at Greenwich to discuss terms. For this encounter, Henry commanded an extravaganza which required *two* halls to be built in the tiltyard – one for the banquet and one for an accompanying masque. Hans Holbein himself designed the triumphal arch which connected the two rooms. The banqueting hall was one hundred feet long and had a frieze around the tops of the walls depicting 'fights between savages and beasts', while a balcony over the centre span of Holbein's arch contained a troupe of musicians who played as the guests ate. The ceiling of the masque hall was painted with the signs of the zodiac, the planets and a map of the world. Scenery and costumes for the masque alone cost in the region of £8,000, and the whole event was of unparalleled magnificence. Did it have any effect on negotiations? It's hard to say: except that Francis I didn't marry Mary, but did marry the widow of the king of Portugal, in 1530.

There is no modern equivalent of this mixture of state business and sheer personal profligacy; any more than there is an equivalent of the kind royal township which Greenwich had become by this stage. Even the world's richest and most despotic rulers find it hard to divert a nation's wealth towards such monumental frivolities in the way that Henry did. And yet, even as royal life at Greenwich reached this apogee of ostentation, it started to turn sour. It happened once Anne Boleyn had made her appearance, and the whole unexpected and largely unintended business of the Reformation, driven by Henry's obsession with divorce and the struggle to produce a male heir, began to take over.

Finally divorced from Catherine of Aragon, Henry secretly married Anne in 1533. In September of the same year a daughter was born at Greenwich Palace: the future Queen Elizabeth I. In a final excess of enthusiasm for Greenwich, Henry had the palace refurbished. He extended the kitchens, let in new windows in the royal apartments, adorned the ceilings with new bosses, reglazed, repaved, retiled, repainted and repanelled. Elizabeth was christened in the church abutting (indeed, an effective part of) Greenwich Palace – a house of Franciscan observant friars, who had been living there in humble poverty since the end of the previous century and who had baptised Henry VIII and married him to Catherine of Aragon.

But the friars were beginning to make trouble for the licentious – and, to them, blasphemous – king and court next door. Despite erratic attempts at *rapprochement* by the king, they persisted in denouncing sins in high places, and refused to acknowledge Henry as the supreme head of the Church – a title he had assumed in 1534. After threatening to have one of the friars sewn up in a sack and thrown into the Thames – following a particularly public row in church – Henry finally lost patience with them, arrested, tortured and killed a number of them, and dissolved the monastery in 1536. According to contemporary accounts, this provocative decision engendered an outbreak of evil omens: a comet was seen, the River Thames flooded the palace chapel, a whale was caught at Greenwich, and the whole court was stricken by the deadly sweating sickness.

But by now Greenwich had to share the king's affections with its rival Hampton Court, and with the new St James's Palace being constructed in the heart of London. And the nightmare of Henry's later years was starting to take hold. In 1536 he had Anne Boleyn executed and in the same year married Jane Seymour, who bore him his son, Edward – to reign briefly as Edward VI – but who died shortly after childbirth. In 1540 he married Anne of Cleves at Greenwich, by proxy; but discovered, on actually meeting her a few days later, that she was markedly less appealing than Holbein's portrait of her had suggested (when he rowed to Rochester to greet her for the first time, he cried out, 'I will not be married to that Flanders mare!'). Henry divorced her in the same year. Catherine Howard followed, but was beheaded as a punishment for her alleged promiscuity. His sixth wife, Catherine Parr, saw the king into his grave: and when he died, in 1547, the greatest days of royal Greenwich died with him, lost in the madness and distraction of his final years.

What happened after Henry's death? The ailing Edward VI evidently had some feeling for his father's palace. In 1551, aged fourteen, he held (in his own words) a 'Grett tryumphe at Grenwyche', in the course of which there was a 'Chaleng at running at ring'. The sickly king did not do well: 'The price was of my side lost.' He enjoyed visiting the dockyards and watching naval displays – to such an extent that the High Street of Deptford had to be paved over at a cost of £88, as it was 'so noiysome and full of fylth that the Kinges Majestie might not pass to a fro to see ye buylding of His shippes' Finally, he retreated to Greenwich to try and recover from his lingering consumption, but without success. He was forced to quell rumours of his early demise by sitting, propped up and feverish at a palace window, where people walking beside the river could see him. A quack physician prolonged his life for three weeks by giving him arsenic to stanch the flow of consumptive blood; but inevitably he died, in such a state from the slow poisoning which had been administered to him that when the Lord Mayor of

London was summoned to Greenwich on the boy's death (and he was only sixteen years old) the body was too disfigured to be shown. A horrible end for the gilded child painted by Holbein in 1539.

After Edward's death, Mary I and Elizabeth both had their uses for Greenwich Palace – Mary rather less than her sister. Hardly surprising, perhaps, since her reign lasted a mere five years to Elizabeth's forty-four; and since on one of her infrequent visits to the palace someone managed to fire a cannonball (intended as a salute) through the wall of her apartment, 'to the great terror of herself and her ladies'.

Elizabeth made Greenwich her principal summer residence, despite a remorseless peripatetic schedule. Shifting from Greenwich to Richmond, to Hampton Court, to the Palace of Westminster, and further out into the rest of the country, she would impose herself restlessly on her wealthier subjects. Queen Elizabeth's Oak, more or less in the centre of Greenwich Park (and actually dead for over a hundred years), is supposedly the tree under which she most liked to take her ease. And it was at Greenwich, in a piece of typically Elizabethan theatre, that she reinstated the Maundy ceremony – the practice of washing the feet of the poor on the Thursday before Good Friday: a ceremony with surprisingly Catholic overtones for such a fervent Protestant as Elizabeth. Nevertheless, in 1572 she brought the institution back to life, and personally washed the feet of thirty-nine paupers (one for each year of her age) – after making sure that these same feet had already been well washed beforehand. Indeed, they were more than well washed – they were positively pampered. First, the Yeoman of the Laundry came out with a silver basin filled with warm water and flowers, washed, wiped and kissed the feet of the thirty-nine poor, then made the sign of the cross just above the toes of each one. After him, the Almoner – the royal officer in charge of distributing alms – did the same. Finally the queen appeared, and after psalms and prayers, did the same again, attended by thirty-nine ladies and gentlemen bearing aprons and towels. She also distributed the Maundy gifts, or Royal Maunds – the predecessors of the current monarch's Maundy Money. Among other things, the Elizabethan paupers got enough broadcloth for a gown, a pair of shoes, a wooden platter covered with fish and a purse containing thirty-nine pieces of money. What can they have made of it, the emergence – as if from Heaven – of this gracious, terrifying figure, suddenly bending low and kissing their newly fragrant feet?

Then there was more theatre: it was here that Sir Walter Raleigh laid his cloak over a puddle (allegedly over the mud of the Woolwich Road, which at the time bisected Greenwich Park) so that the queen should not soil her shoes. And here, in 1572, Elizabeth reviewed an army of 1,400 men which had been raised by the City of London in response to a plot (involving the Duke of Norfolk) to overthrow her and reinstate Mary Queen of Scots. For this event, a mock battle was staged, 'which had all the appearances of a regular battle except for the spilling of blood'.

Elizabeth used the proximity of Greenwich Palace to the dockyards in Deptford and Woolwich to keep an eye on Britain's growing naval presence and affirm her political and international purpose by outward display. Seamen such as Sir Martin Frobisher (off in search of the North-West Passage in 1576) would sail downriver from Deptford for a farewell audience with the queen and then head for the open sea; while others, such as the piratical Francis Drake, returned there after their voyagings. It was at Deptford that Elizabeth knighted Drake after his astonishing (and profitable – he came back with £1 million of Spanish gold) circumnavigation of the globe, which lasted from December 1577 to September 1580. The ceremony took place aboard his ship *The Golden Hind*, anchored at Deptford after Drake had sailed up the Thames, firing his guns in salute to the queen – to be repaid by a royal wave from a palace window – and was performed with a gilded sword at a vast banquet, in the presence of crowds of wildly enthusiastic subjects. *The Golden Hind*, incidentally, stayed at Deptford for the rest of its days, kept on view at a special dock, until eventually it rotted away in the water.

And it was at Greenwich that Elizabeth saw the beacon lit on Shooters Hill to announce the sighting of the Spanish Armada, and where she signed the orders to repel the threatened invasion. Following that, she crossed the river to Tilbury to address a land force of 2,000 men, sent there to guard the queen at Greenwich, with the words, 'I know I have the body of a weak and feeble woman, but I have the heart and stomach of a king . . .' So the palace, and Greenwich as a whole, acquired a patina of Elizabethan distinction, even if royal patronage was on nothing like the scale of the days of Henry VIII. Elizabethan Greenwich was an assemblage of acts and events; moments in the reign which kept Greenwich alive as a principal contender for the favours and attentions of the monarchy.

But after that?

When Elizabeth died, in 1603, James VI of Scotland and I of England assumed the throne. Clearly he had less interest in Greenwich than any of his Tudor predecessors. The site of Whitehall Palace was much more appealing to him, so he got Inigo Jones and John Webb to draw up plans for a huge new palace on the same spot. Out-of-town Greenwich (and London by this stage was becoming a real metropolis) went to his wife, the frivolous and spendthrift Anne of Denmark, the gift being formalised in 1614: 'In consideration of our conjugal love etc., we grant to Queen Anne the capital messuage in East Greenwich called Greenwich House, with the Friers there, the gardens, orchards, etc., with Greenwich Park, and the houses and lodges within the park . . .' While this was still something worth possessing (and the gift to Queen Anne reduced Henry Howard, Earl of Northampton, to despair, since he thought he'd legally bought the place in 1604) the rest of Greenwich was suffering from a marked falling-off. Records describe the main streets of post-Tudor Greenwich as 'loathsome, dangerous and infectious'; while the parish church was in a state of near-ruin, with its steeple about to collapse. When Queen Anne assumed owner-ship of Greenwich Palace, it was clear that the life had rather gone out of the rest of the neighbourhood.

So what remains of all that staggering Tudor energy and invest-ment, from Duke Humphrey to Queen Elizabeth, nearly two hundred years of frenetic activity? Where can you best get a sense of that time? Even Greenwich Park itself was heavily altered in appearance in the seventeenth century, from Tudor chase to something much more urbane and park-like. Is there anything left? Is there anything, even, from the early Jacobean years?

The best you can do is probably to leave Greenwich itself and go a mile or so eastwards, to Charlton. Nowadays just another stop on the railway line, a part of the sprawl of outer London, Charlton once possessed quite a substantial early British settle-ment (two thousand years ago), occupying the site of what is now Maryon Park. It was big enough and important enough to have been named, as Cerletone, in the Domesday Book. And it has, to its great and inexplicable glory, one of the most stunning pieces of Jacobean architecture in the whole country, perched in its dead centre.

This is Charlton House. Dating from 1607, it has a tangential, but real, royal connection: it was the home of Adam Newton, the Dean of Durham and tutor to Prince Henry, eldest son of James I and heir to the throne. It is the most wonderful building, made all the more wonderful by the drabness of its surroundings. To get to it from the run-down concrete shell of Charlton railway station means walking south along Charlton Church Lane, with Victorian converted bedsitters on one side, a startling grey new brutalist block of flats on the other, and only the odd passing car on the way to the Woolwich Road to remind you that life does actually go on. After five minutes of uninspiring foot-slogging, you reach the brow of the hill: a redbrick church – St Luke's, the 'Charlton Church' of the lane – on the left; ranks of flats on the right; and in the centre, hemmed in by a car park and a stretch of lawn, a fabulous dark red brick Jacobean mansion, decorated with white stone quoins and dressings, and with a great wedding-cake frontispiece, involving a huge bay window and the main entrance porch. Sir Nikolaus Pevsner claimed that Charlton House contained 'the most exuberant and undisciplined ornament in all England'; while Ian Nairn, in a moment of typical indulgence, compared it to 'a stray from some Baltic waterfront', before converting this comparison into a metaphor drawn – aptly enough – from Jacobean melodrama, seeing the building as 'Sinister poetry: Duchess of Malfi, S.E.17'.

It is remarkable, not just because of its apparent completeness (most buildings of a similar vintage have either been knocked down or severely disfigured by later architectural additions) or because of its wonderful paired towers, roaring lion faces, or curlicued brackets. It's also remarkable because of its setting on top of the hill, which gives you a feeling of what it might have been like for Adam Newton, four centuries ago. To the east lies Charlton Park, originally the grounds of the house, now a public park (opened in 1929) and bearing a predictable mixture of playing-fields, goalposts, distant tower blocks and looming cranes. To the west is the fairly trafficky Charlton Road, some between-the-wars housing, more blocks of flats and, in between, something magical: a glimpse of the Thames winding westward round the promontory of North Greenwich and the Millennium Dome, seemingly miles below. You get a sudden sense of how high up you are, with the Thames distant at your feet, and how the parkland at the back of the house must have been the most splendid high, open space, a real delight. John Evelyn, writing some fifty years after Charlton House was built, described the view from the house as 'one of the most noble in the world, for city, river, ships, meadows, hill, woods and all other amenities'.

The architect was almost certainly John Thorpe, and the construction of Charlton House lasted from 1607 to 1612 – the year in which Prince Henry died, never having seen the house completed. Newton, fortunately for him, carried on in the employment of James I, before dying in 1629. After various changes of ownership it passed into the hands of the Maryon-Wilson family, who enjoyed it from 1767 to 1923, at which point it became the property of the old Metropolitan Borough of Greenwich, before finally becoming what it is today: council community centre, library and park.

This is clearly something of an embarrassment for the council, who are happy to keep Charlton House on as a meeting place for the people of Woolwich, but evidently wish that it wasn't quite such an architecturally distinguished place. If the National Trust ever got their hands on it, they would make it one of London's historical stars – heavily promoted and almost certainly refurbished (the layers of gloss paint, the tables and chairs, the gloomy curtains all removed) and filled with borrowed period furnishings. But the London Borough of Greenwich is caught in an uneasy clinch between finances, tourism and preservation – a clinch which at the moment affects an awful lot of historical Greenwich.

It *is* possible to visit Charlton House, usually as part of a guided tour, and it's certainly easy enough to look at the outside, or to sneak a peek at the old chapel and the Wilson Room, since these have been turned into a lending library. But the best thing is to get access on your own to the interior; because then it becomes clear how rich Charlton House is, and how expressive of a particular moment in taste, a moment when the Gothic tradition, which had sustained English architecture, with endless variation, from the twelfth century all the way through to the Tudor Gothic that Henry VIII would have known, finally gave way to continental influences and began to play with Renaissance, classically inspired forms, and even some of the exaggerated mannerist habits of sixteenth-century Italian architecture. So the brickwork and foursquareness lead back to, say,

Hampton Court; while the decoration, the absence of Gothic arches, the classical faces and forms dotted around, all lead forward to the new age.

You can watch the struggle inside as you go from room to room. In the Percival Room on the first floor is a beautiful plasterwork ceiling, interlocking rings as a variation of standard Jacobean strapwork with tiny pendants – the incredibly distant cousins of the pendant vaulting in Christ Church Cathedral, Oxford – that look like fruits waiting to be plucked. This, along with the room's stone-mullioned windows and bay window, feel pretty much part of the preceding century. But then you press on up the stairs (layers of institutional paintwork on the walls, fantastical faces and tropical foliage carved into the newel posts) to the Long Gallery and two things happen. You are stunned by the loveliness of the room – big, a real gentleman's space, but not so huge as to be intimidating or unusable; and you can see how change is creeping in, in the forms of the little plaster men on the ceiling (fronds of leaves for lower bodies; insect wings poking out of their backs) and the little classical marble fireplace.

On a bit more to the Grand Salon, and another stunning ceiling – strapwork and pendants, the royal arms by one window, the Prince of Wales feathers by another – acres of light and space, and a completely mad fireplace again, all Corinthian pilasters and with two large nude figures, over four feet tall, propping up the mantel. These are, in fact, Vulcan and Venus: Vulcan staring up at the magnificent ceiling, Venus smiling coyly in his general direction. Given that they were man and wife but that she was persistently adulterous, their apparent lack of communication is understandable.

And then back down the stairs with their bizarre carvings ('The wooden heads yawn and jeer,' as the writer Iain Sinclair puts it) until at the bottom you end up face to face with the medieval figures of a boar's head and a stag, carved on the doors to the chapel and the Wilson Room. The boar is emblematic of Newton's family; the stag standing for the Puckerings, the family of Newton's wife. Two worlds again – the reforming Renaissance, Vulcan and Venus, and the declining Jacobean traditional, boar's heads and stags. This is as near as you're going to get, in Greenwich, to a taste of what once was: primitive, curiously sweet, homespun and sophisticated, all in one building. The final inheritance of Tudor style, the closing of a chapter in architecture.

At least it would be, except for one strange outbuilding in the grounds. As you come back out of the porch, with the old gateway stranded on the lawn in front of you, to the right, tucked gloomily into a shrubbery, is a square brick building with a curious sloping pagoda-like roof. It turns out to be a public lavatory: one designed, believe it or not, by Inigo Jones. The accepted view is that it was once a summerhouse, dating from around 1630 and bearing the hallmarks of the man who was to lead a revolution in taste two miles west, back in Greenwich proper.

*

In June 1617 John Chamberlain wrote to Sir Dudley Carleton a letter from which Greenwich enthusiasts love to quote. He wrote that the queen 'is building somewhat at Greenwich which must be finished this summer; it is said to be some curious device of Inigo Jones, and will cost above £4,000'. The 'curious device' turned out to be the Queen's House, one of the most influential buildings ever constructed in England. This would be the great precursor of centuries of English classicism, that peculiarly reticent adaptation of Palladianism which the English turned out to have a genius for, and which still informs many of our ideas about form, proportion, correctness and harmony in architecture. And it started in Greenwich, with Inigo Jones's cunning scheme to bridge the Woolwich Road (the one where Raleigh had extended his cape for Queen Elizabeth), allowing the queen to cross from one half of the park to the other in order and complete privacy; and at the same time, to create a new kind of building, a cultural statement that no one would be able to ignore.

So who was Inigo Jones? Born in London in the 1570s, he came from a humble enough background – his father was a clothworker, also called Inigo, and he probably trained as a joiner. Although his early life is obscure, it's evident that by the time he was in his thirties he had travelled extensively in Italy and was starting to perfect his skills as a painter and designer. He first came to public notice in England in the early 1600s, when he was employed by Queen Anne to design scenes and costumes for the masques she loved to watch – spectacular, elaborate entertainments with music, poetry and startling stage effects: ships at sea, battles, gods descending on chariots from the sky. The great dramatist and poet, Ben Jonson, supplied the texts for many of Jones's masques, among them *Oberon, the Fairy Prince*, from which we get: 'Buzz quoth the blue flie, Hum quoth the bee.'

But Jones had ambitions for more than just stage tricks, however technically stunning. He became the King's Surveyor of Works in 1615, after revisiting Italy in the two preceding years, a time crucial to his development as an architect: in this period he fell under the influence of the great sixteenth-century Italian architect, Andrea Palladio, and he developed his passion for classicism. So when the queen gave him his first really big commission, for the Greenwich house in 1616, he was bursting with creativity and enthusiasm for what would be a completely new look, a look so modern, so avant-garde that no other building in England would come close to it. Drawing his inspiration from the Poggio a Caiano, the Medici villa near Florence, but giving it a more Palladian twist, he came up with a breathtakingly cool, H-shaped building (the centre of the H being the bridge room across the Woolwich Road), a classical loggia on the south side, a curving double staircase to the north, and the most brilliantly restrained classical detailing overall. Jones himself described the exterior as 'Sollid, proporsionable according to the rules, masculine and unaffected.'

Of course, there were problems – not least the fact that Queen Anne died in 1619, well before the house was finished. Work came to a halt, thatch was quickly put over the top to keep the weather out (there was no roof), and the shell sat there, waiting for an upturn in its fortunes. This duly arrived in 1629, when the new king, Charles I, gave the house to his queen, Henrietta Maria, who asked Jones to finish the building. It took another six years to complete the exterior, and another five years after that before the interior was more or less done – although beautifications were still in hand when the Civil War broke out in 1642. But it was, in essence, finished by 1640, and the queen called it her 'House of Delights'. It is a wonderful building. Even though it's now dwarfed from the river by the Royal Naval College, and its pure classical lines (with the colonnades on either side dating from the nineteenth century) look pretty but familiar, and the heavy lorries on the Romney Road snub it every time they rumble past – even though things have changed all around it, and it can look hopelessly small and isolated, it is still a wonderful building. You can see just how wonderful it is if you compare it with its close contemporary, Charlton House.

After all, what separates the two? A decade, from the moment when building started on Charlton, to the moment when building started on the Queen's House: no time at all. Yet the difference between the two is the difference between a flying boat and Concorde. Charlton House doesn't stop being delightful when you compare it with the Queen's House; it's just as charming and quirky as ever. But its bricks and stones and massive windows and fantastical ornamentation suddenly look agricultural in comparison with Inigo Jones's pared-down classical elegance. Yet public reaction to the Jones design at first tended to dismiss it as over-refined royal whimsy. The cultured classes on whom it was to make its initial impact saw it as a stage set, a masque backdrop which happened to be brick and stone, but which was really no more permanent than if it had been made of painted wood. And in comparison with a doughty presence like Charlton House, it *does* look light and ephemeral. There's a brief glimpse of it under construction, in a seventeenth-century Flemish painting, a *Prospect of London and the Thames from above Greenwich*: you can just make it out, two frail little whitish blocks waiting to be joined up like some sort of Wendy house, with the huge red-brown bulk of the old Greenwich Palace looming up behind it – a *real* building, not a dandified theatrical toy. The fact that this plaything was about to usher in an approach to architecture that would revolutionise the appearance of England was neither here nor there. People were sceptical.

In a way you can see why, when you go round the interior of the Queen's House. The recent restorations – done in the 1980s – have left it so perfect and white and immaculate that it doesn't quite seem like a real house, a place where anyone, even a queen, might have lived. Its formal tidiness resists the human touch – unlike Charlton House, where every surface has been used and worn, and where the presence of human life is immediately obvious, not least in the Minstrel Hall, filled with people drinking cafeteria coffee and puffing cheerfully away at cigarettes.

But the Queen's House is nonetheless incontrovertibly beautiful, outside and in – especially the Great Hall, the central feature of the house and a perfect 40-foot cube. This has been fiddled around with by succeeding generations – the casement doors to the terrace were altered in the eighteenth century, while the windows on to the central roadway were adjusted as part of a reconstruction in the 1930s. What's more, the statuary and the gorgeous ceiling paintings are all modern reproductions: enormous photographic reprints, in the case of the paintings. Even so, the dimensions remain as before, and the incredible, profligate use of space – all that empty air, doing nothing useful at all! – combine to make a room that's not just advanced for the seventeenth century, but which is still astonishingly modern.

Back in Charlton House, the Grand Salon is big and filled with light as well – but it's a lovely period piece. The Great Hall of the Queen's House, on the other hand, is absolutely outside time – as, in their way, are the Tulip Stairs that lead off from one corner. They're called the Tulip Stairs because the wrought-iron balustrade which coils up with them has, predictably, a repeated tulip motif. But what's really astonishing about this stone staircase is the way it's cantilevered from the wall, with no visible means of support. It is unbelievably pure, simple and modern. After Charlton's crazy old wooden staircase, with its yowling faces, its vegetation and cabbalistic pierced pyramids, these stairs – the first cantilevered stairs built in this country – look space age.

*

Naturally, they're helped by the way they've been painted in pure white paint, with the tulip balustrade in blue – almost an Yves Klein blue in some lights. The loving 1980s restoration has helped to emphasise the geometrical purity of the structure. But then this becomes a central issue in our whole appreciation of the Queen's House: the way it's been conserved. After all, what happened to it once Queen Henrietta Maria had moved in, in 1629? We know that the queen furnished the house as extravagantly as possible – one sycophantic visitor claimed that 'It far surpasseth all other of that kind in England' – and that there she gave birth to a son, Charles James, who died shortly afterwards, the last royal child to be born at Greenwich. We also know that in 1642 she left it, in order to raise funds for the Royalist cause in the Civil War, and that by the end of that year it had been taken from royal keeping.

After that, the works of art which the queen had carefully amassed were sold off, and the house was used for, among other things, the lying-in-state of Parliamentarian generals. Come the Restoration in 1660, however, and the house was given a fresh lease of life when Charles II had it enlarged. Two more bridge rooms were added and the interior plan slightly altered, so that he and his queen, Catherine of Braganza, could comfortably use it – the old Greenwich Palace, the Placentia of a hundred and fifty years earlier, being semi-derelict by this stage. Between 1660 and 1665 some £75,000 went on reviving and improving the Queen's House. At the same time, the king decided to smarten up the park, calling in the French landscapist, André le Nôtre, to do the design work. Le Nôtre had made a name for himself with the parks of the château Vaux-le-Vicomte, and was without a doubt the most fashionable garden designer of the day. A whole new scheme involving elms and Spanish chestnuts converging on the house was laid out by Sir William Boreman, but there's no positive evidence that le Nôtre himself ever turned up to superintend the work.

As it turned out, it was Charles's mother, Henrietta Maria, who settled briefly back into her old house, rather than the king, who never got round to using it. She did this in style: twenty-four gentlemen wearing black velvet suits attended her public appearances, while a dozen uniformed bargemen rowed her up and down the Thames, from Greenwich to Denmark House, her residence in London. But after that? A certain decline begins to make itself apparent. The house had various lodgers (including John Flamsteed, the first Astronomer Royal), before the Earl of Dorset, Ranger of Greenwich Park, took it over. His successor, the Earl of Romney, made a significant change by diverting the main road from under the building and re-routing to the south – the present-day Romney Road. A room was also built underneath the central bridge of the house, blocking the old roadway and linking the two sections of the house at ground level. These two alterations alone must have made a huge difference to the liveability of the place. No matter how far you were from the road, and how well curtained and carpeted the room, the racket from thousands of horses' hooves clattering past a few feet below, plus the smell of horse dung (to say nothing of the noise of the common folk, quite possibly passing critical remarks about the inhabitants of the building), must have been appalling. Diverting the Woolwich road south was Lord Romney's great gift to the Queen's House. His successor, Sir William Gifford, made no real improvements; instead he fiddled around doing repairs and altering the fastidious line of Inigo Jones's ground floor windows.

By now we are into the eighteenth century, which is where the rot really starts to set in. Lady Catherine Pelham (wife of the Prime Minister, Henry Pelham) became park ranger (basically a grace and favour title attached to the park) and used the Queen's House mainly for entertaining. After her death in 1780, the house lapsed into the ownership of various members of the royal family, in the course of which a positively negligent housekeeper was installed and overall control seemed to disintegrate. By 1792 the place was not only being used as the headquarters of a successful smuggling ring but had gone so far downhill that the housekeeper and her husband were accused of making 'a hog-stye of the house and a cow-house of the premises'.

A few years later, and all formal royal connections came to an end when the house was bought (in 1806) from Caroline, Princess of Wales, and was turned over to the Royal Naval Asylum School. Previously in Paddington, this was a boarding-school for sailors' orphans. At once building work began, to add east and west wings to house the school's 950 charges, while the interior of the house was radically worked over to create five staff residences and some dormitories for the pupils. An architect called Daniel Alexander was in charge of the design, and the work went on from 1807 to 1816. None too badly, you might think, looking at the outside: Alexander's colonnades follow the line of the old Woolwich Road and look every bit as chaste and well formed as Jones's central masterpiece.

But however much money went on the additions and alterations, it was still a pretty rough way for the Queen's House to end up. If you put the best part of a thousand boys in one place and keep them there for over a century (the school, incidentally, changed its name to the Royal Hospital School after it merged in 1821 with the Greenwich Hospital School – previously in the Queen Anne block of the Royal Naval Hospital – and finally moved out to Suffolk in 1933) then you are going to end up with something entirely without regality. Pictures taken in the school's heyday show tough-looking lads in britches and caps playing a vigorous game of cricket on the lawns just below Jones's graceful double staircase; or boys standing in matelot uniforms around the main gates, with the house in the background and an immense landlocked training ship, *Fame*, standing in front of it, where it had been specially built; or the interior of the Great Hall, the exquisitely, mathematically refined Great Hall, covered in dark paint and with a heavy varnished roll call of the dead from the First World War stuck up on the wall: Lest We Forget. Elsewhere, partitions had been put up, walls had been knocked through, staircases squeezed in, bathrooms and fireplaces haphazardly inserted. The fabric had been, effectively, mauled.

And then, the twentieth century. After all this – this cycle of building, embellishment and neglect – the Queen's House has been pretty thoroughly traduced. So when the Office of Works gets hold of it, in the mid-1930s, it does its best to peel away some of the damage of time and schoolboys, and turns the building into the central portion of the National Maritime Museum. In 1984 another restoration programme gets under way which lasts six more years and is a concerted attempt to try and bring the house back to something like its original – 1660s – state.

The finished effect is very odd: this conserved beauty, this very end-of-the-century discretion. The house is left in a sort of limbo, not really of the seventeenth century, and somehow oddly anticipating the twentieth. That Great Hall, with its extravagant emptiness; that Tulip Staircase, with its blue and white colour scheme and its fabulous spiralling geometry: both look modern, but they can't be. Whereas the King's Presence Chamber, a stunning blue room on the first floor, looks old, but is in fact almost brand new – painstakingly reconstituted. The only original bits are the cornice, the frieze and the ceiling beams; everything else has been remade or acquired from somewhere else. The gilt has been redone and the gorgeous blue of the walls, although based on traces of Inigo Jones's original paintwork (done with a material called smalt, a pigment made with crushed glass to produce a sparkling effect), is also new. The King's Anteroom has an authentic carved wooden ceiling – the Navy actually tried to hijack Inigo Jones's carvers to work on the huge *Sovereign of the Seas* being built for Charles I at Woolwich – but a repro fireplace. Similarly, the Queen's Presence Chamber, done in a magisterial wine-red, has antique Brussels tapestries, but a reproduction chimneypiece and new silk damask made from a seventeenth-century pattern.

The rest of the house is pretty bare, save for some representative oil paintings and one or two illustrative sticks of furniture, all of which makes much more of an impression than the rooms that have been dressed up to look the part. Everywhere there are perfect white walls, coir fitted carpets, matt grey doors and a few clever little low-key artificial candles, lit by fibre optics. This is minimalism, exactly the kind of minimalism that fans like to enthuse about – proof that minimal style is nothing new, but an expression of something specific to the English character, something which has been asserting itself for centuries. Look at the way, you could argue, that the Queen's House lends itself to the pared-down treatment: it fits it perfectly. What's more, minimal style looks bare but is actually an expensive, refined, involved way of doing things; an aristocrat of styles. So it's appropriate – quite accidentally – that the house, having been stripped of possessions and integrity over the years, should come back to life in such a modern, autocratic form. Indeed, if you took two rooms to compare and contrast, between Charlton House and the Queen's

House, you could do worse than to pick Charlton's Grand Salon, which, despite being filled with contemporary bits of council furniture (a large meeting-table and a mass of stacking chairs), is still evidently an early seventeenth-century room, slightly crude in the details, but absolutely rich with period feel; and, say, the Queen's Outer Closet, which the queen's attendants (Mistress of the Robes; Ladies of the Bedchamber) would have used, and which is now restored to an utterly timeless modern simplicity, with a single fibre-optic candle, a simple wooden bed (in a markedly Scandinavian style), a cream blanket, a bare fireplace, empty white-panelled walls, and curtainless rectangular windows. For better or worse, this is what Inigo Jones's creation has become – a piece of pure design.

So whatever happened to the royalty? The sparse interiors curiously mirror the vanishing trick performed by England's monarchs over the years after Charles II. They simply didn't live at Greenwich any more, and their legacy became more and more a matter of historical recollection, and less and less of actual presence. Of course there was the Royal Observatory to come, in 1675, Charles II's gift to the world, built with Wren's assistance. And there was the great Royal Naval Hospital – which was really a kind of accident, in that what began as a new palace for Charles lapsed due to a loss of royal interest in the project, and only took on a life of its own and became the great visual symbol of Greenwich when Queen Mary II revived the scheme with the intention of turning it into a home for seamen. Her royal authority is stamped all over it, not just because she ordered it to be built, but because she ordered it to be built in such a way that the Queen's House would still enjoy its view of the waterfront. The royal prerogative made bricks and stone.

But Mary didn't live at the Queen's House, any more than Charles II did. She and King William much preferred Hampton Court – on which they lavished huge sums of money – and Kensington Palace, to which they also devoted considerable time, money and energy. It was all in keeping with a general move west – something that London has been doing as a whole, ever since the Romans arrived – leaving Greenwich stranded out on the estuary. Throughout the eighteenth century, St James's Palace was the principal royal residence in London, while Queen Victoria established Buckingham Palace as her preferred London base, with Windsor Castle, Balmoral, Sandringham and Osborne as country retreats. Indeed, by the twentieth century the appearance of the monarch in Greenwich was so occasional that it came to be a special event: such as when George VI came down in 1937, along with his mother, Queen Mary, to open the National Maritime Museum in the old Queen's House; or when Queen Elizabeth II copied her forebear, Elizabeth I, and came to Greenwich to knight Sir Francis Chichester after his solo circumnavigation of the globe with the same sword that Elizabeth I had used on Sir Francis Drake.

*

So this is why Greenwich is the way it is. A kind of whirlwind of royal interest and patronage, which touched down shortly after Duke Humphrey established his base here in the fifteenth century, reached a climax with Henry VIII and then drifted slowly off, over the next hundred and fifty years. Something fantastic has been left behind (and it's just possible there may be bits of Placentia lying under the Royal Naval College, but only if Wren missed them when he demolished the old palace in 1694), but of the monarchy itself, not an awful lot. Greenwich owes its architectural heritage, its historical riches, to a royal caprice, a two-hundred-year fascination which blew up and then faded away entirely. It's hard to think of anywhere else where this has happened quite so conclusively: the royal residences of Balmoral, Sandringham, Windsor, Buckingham Palace, Kensington Palace and St James's Palace all get regular use. It is possible for the royal family to maintain an interest after the first flush of enthusiasm has worn off. But not in south-east London.

Maybe the nearest approximation to Greenwich is the Tower of London – gradually eclipsed as a royal residence once the great move upriver towards Westminster and Whitehall had begun – last used for the traditional overnight stay before the day of coronation by Charles II. It, too, is stuck in the east; it, too, is surrounded by unsympathetic latterday buildings; it, too, is a tourist hub, rather than a royal resource; it, too, is magnificent and free of royals. A curious conjunction.

MARITIME II

WHEN THE National Maritime Museum opened in Greenwich in 1937, it looked as if it was trying to fuse two strands of Greenwich history – sea and royalty, just like the old days of Henry VIII. Co-opting the old Royal Naval Asylum School for the museum's premises meant co-opting the Queen's House at the same time, even though the house's main connection with maritime affairs was the fact that it interrupted the line of Wren's Royal Naval Hospital when seen from the water. Still, the inhabitants of the Asylum School departed, the Office of Works restored the queen's former home, the wings of the old school were smartened up and the huge gymnasium built in 1873 between the west wing and the new wing became the Neptune Hall – aptly enough, with its scallop shell crowning the entrance, its sea creatures and its antique vessels above the paired pillars to either side of the arched gateway.

In fact, there was already a tradition at Greenwich – hardly surprisingly – of collecting museum-worthy maritime artefacts and memorabilia. The Royal Naval College had been amassing paintings for decades, and by 1850 had opened its own National Gallery of Naval Art, with over 300 portraits and paintings of naval actions: the first of its kind in the world. At the start of the twentieth century there were moves to upgrade this into a full-blown maritime museum, led by the redoubtable Sir James Caird, a Scottish shipowner with a passion for maritime history. Caird was not only a driving force in establishing the new national museum; he also provided it with gifts amounting to £1.25 million – a sum worth about £100 million in today's money. However, the new collection really got going with the addition of a private hoard of over 11,000 objects, acquired from a Mr A. G. H. Macpherson. By 1929, another private collection – of models of almost every type of British sailing craft made since the sixteenth century – had been added, and King George V and Queen Mary had both made significant donations. Once the government had decided officially to back the new National Maritime Museum, items flooded in from all over the world – including Sir Francis Drake's astrolabe, plus the 1,000-volume archives from the Royal Naval Dockyards at Chatham. And when George VI (enthroned in 1936) spoke the words, 'I am glad that the opening of this museum should be one of the first cere-monies of my reign', he was putting the royal imprimatur on the largest and most important maritime museum in the world.

Now, was this a just recognition of Greenwich's place in the great maritime history of the nation? The logical culmination of centuries of tradition? Or was it a recognition that Greenwich and the water had been parting company for years and – despite the presence of the Royal Naval College – an acknowledgement of the fact that it was now a place for museums rather than ships? Was it optimistic? Or was it an admission of defeat?

When Henry established the first naval dockyard at Deptford at the start of the sixteenth century, he started something remarkable. Deptford and Woolwich, the two hard-working towns either side of Greenwich, swiftly became nationally important – with Deptford assuming the position of most important dockyard on the Thames, beating off strong local competition from Chatham, further out in the estuary. Before long, the Royal Naval Dockyard at Deptford covered 30 acres and was a sprawling mess of workers, warships and materials. It had five slipways, single and double dry docks for building – and huge piles of timber. Much of this wood was simply left to rot away and fall to pieces, owing to the working practices of the day, and to the fact that no one had worked out a satisfactory way to store timber long term and keep it in good condition. It wasn't until 1772 that the dockyard took on new ideas about wood seasoning and ventilation to preserve its principal raw material. Even when it did, it still had to grapple with age-old problems of theft and corruption – problems which had always bedevilled the yard with its rackety system of payments, which positively drove yard workers to larceny, and its half-baked security arrangements. The famously scrupulous (and parsimonious) Samuel Pepys found 'Much evidence of neglect' in 1661 and spent the rest of the decade complaining to the king about pilfering. He even tried to institute new arrangements to halt the chronic theft of equipment and material supplies, but without much success.

Despite all this, Deptford grew to be the dockyard with the highest output of naval ships in the country, and was so renowned that in 1697 Peter the Great, Tsar of Russia, came to study its methods and work in the yards. This was in the course of Peter's famous progress around Europe, his radical plan to garner ideas and information from all the most up-to-date countries, import them into Russia and modernise the whole country. The Great Progress was the first trip abroad by a reigning tsar in peacetime. And since Deptford's prestige had spread throughout Europe, Peter, who was mad about boats, decided to spend time there, acquire some of the shipwright's skills at first hand, learn about seamanship and explore the latest trends in navigation.

At least, that was the idea. Unfortunately the twenty-five-year-old ruler spent an undue amount of time at Deptford getting paralytically drunk with his friends and wrecking John Evelyn's Deptford home, Sayes Court, which he was renting for the duration. If only it had stayed at drunk. Not only did the young Russian gentlemen drink like fishes, they also used portraits hanging in Evelyn's house for target practice, tipped ink and grease over his carpets, broke the door locks and burned every single one of Evelyn's chairs on the fire. On top of that, they high-spiritedly destroyed his carefully tended gardens (including Evelyn's prize holly bushes) with wheelbarrow races and ultimately caused over £350 of damage – which in 1697 was a serious sum.

This, though, was Evelyn's problem, rather than Deptford's. As well as the most important yard in the region, it also became the Royal Navy centre for provisioning when, in 1742, the Navy Board established its official victualling depot just upstream from the dockyard itself – the Victualling Board rapidly becoming known as 'Old Weevil', on account of the staleness of the goods supplied. At first, the main items available were Red House Biscuits – named after the Red House adjoining the victualling yard – but later on Old Weevil also started to handle pickled meat, rum and clothing, all of which, apart from the clothing, were underweight and horrible to the taste.

But by the mid-eighteenth century Deptford was beginning to slide into a new, uneasy, phase. The Thames was silting up. The problem had been spotted back in the seventeenth century, and by the eighteenth the Navy was using a dredger to keep the river navigable at this point. The Napoleonic Wars kept Deptford fully occupied but by the start of the nineteenth century, engineers had concluded that Deptford was too far from the sea, too shallow and too difficult to navigate in to make it worth spending any more money on it. In 1869 the very last ship, the

Druid, was launched at Deptford, and in the same year the yard was closed – along with its sister yard at Woolwich.

Woolwich dockyard had always been somewhat in the shadow of Deptford, despite its (short-lived) triumph with *Great Harry*. Indeed, it had the distinction of constructing the largest vessel in the world – Charles I's *Sovereign of the Seas* – in 1637, and, at £65,586, probably the most expensive. Did this do the Woolwich Dockyard any good in the long run? Any more than the Woolwich Steam Factory, set up midway through the nineteenth century to capitalise on the growth of steamship traffic, helped it through changing times? Clearly not. Woolwich went the same way as Deptford, although not with quite the same ignominious end: once the Deptford dockyard had been shut down, the City Corporation bought up most of what remained and turned it into a cattle market.

The victualling yard did carry on (once Queen Victoria had visited it in 1858 it became the Royal Victoria Victualling Yard – a nice touch of *noblesse oblige* from Her Majesty) for another century, but it too finally closed down, in 1961. And that was very much that for Deptford – which had not even been able to make much income from summer riverboat excursions since the railway had arrived in the mid-nineteenth century. The most naval, most actively maritime part of the Greenwich waterfront, the place where Drake's *Golden Hind* had moored and where Edward VI loved to visit his burgeoning Navy, was now comatose, a muddy strip punctuated by warehouses.

Greenwich has always been a caesura in between the more blue-collar stretches of the shore. With its royal palace, its hotels and inns and day-trippers and later its Royal Naval College, it has never had quite so much remorselessly commercial or workaday naval activity immediately on its doorstep, no matter how intimately connected it has been with the life of the river. And of course the London docks on the opposite bank – East India, Millwall and so on, which had been active since the start of the nineteenth century – made whatever maritime enterprises Greenwich was involved with look relatively small scale, with their 700 acres of enclosed docks, and 1,000 ship arrivals and departures per week. In the first half of the twentieth century, the Greenwich Borough Council, as if to rub home the difference between one world and another, actually spread sand (carefully collected from the seaside) on the strand in front of the Naval College and encouraged people to splash around in the murky Thames waters at low tide. While London still enjoyed its position as the largest, busiest port in the world, contemporary pictures of Greenwich beach show children in bonnets flicking pebbles, large social picnic parties huddling together on the shingle to protect themselves from the English summer, knock-kneed rowing fours overshadowed by the jetty of the LCC power station – all desperately eager to show what a good time they're having, despite the glum weather, the grimy ships moored in midstream, the acres of industrialisation stretching away to either side, on either bank. It was always Greenwich's task to be a little bit more genteel, a place where, ultimately, the biggest single structure on the shore was the power station jetty.

And now the maritime atmosphere is historical, formalised and curated. The river is silent, whichever bank you stand on; and Greenwich has become a place that deals with memories, rather than actualities. When did it start to become like this? What was the key moment? Was it when Lord Nelson died?

The subject of a large and fascinating gallery in the Maritime Museum (with his cut-away breeches and his gruesomely stained stockings preserved like holy relics in a glass case), Nelson is hardly a Greenwich man. The only house he ever owned was on the opposite side of town, in Merton Place, in south-west London; and his most prominent appearance in Greenwich was actually after his death. It was spectacular, though: brought back to Greenwich at the end of 1805, pickled in spirit after the Battle of Trafalgar, borne on the flagship *Victory*, his remains were transported into the great Painted Hall of the Royal Naval Hospital and there placed at the centre of an immense display of sombre morbidity.

Preparations for Nelson's lying-in-state took ten days. Heavy black curtains were hung over the entrance to the hall, while the walls and floor were covered in black cloth, round which ran a contrasting belt of white satin. An elevated dais bore the coffin itself, which was surmounted by a black canopy festooned with gold and ornamented with a triumphal plume. Ten heraldic banners were draped around, and the chaplain of the *Victory* sat as the chief mourner for the three days of the lying-in-state (practically starving himself in the process), accompanied by ten other watchers who flanked the coffin, five on each side.

Anyone visiting Greenwich to pay their respects must have had a powerful theatrical experience. Not only did they have to struggle through interminable crowds to get there; but after hours of patient queuing, suddenly they were face to face with this great silent black tableau, the body of Britain's greatest hero – the man who had thrown back the nation's foes at the Battle of the Nile and at Trafalgar, and who was a romantic legend, to boot – at the absolute centre of this terrible display, the focal point towards which everyone's thoughts and emotions strained. It's the kind of grand, solemn, public memorial that the British can still do conspicuously well, and the mood at Greenwich must have been tangible – not least because so many thousands of people forced their way down from London (in the days before rail) that, according to one estimate, 20,000 mourners had to be turned away on the first day. Huge traffic jams formed all the way back to the centre of town. As *The Times* put it, 'Before eight in the morning every avenue from the metropolis was crowded with vehicles of every description', and 'when the gate was thrown open, above ten thousand persons pressed forward for admittance'.

At the end of the period of public mourning, Nelson's body was taken upriver to St Paul's. At midday on 8 January 1806, his coffin was carried out of the Painted Hall and towards his barge from *Victory*. Five hundred pensioners marched behind, while a fife and drum band played Handel's Dead March. The coffin was placed in the black-shrouded barge, and Nelson's personal crew of forty-six seamen worked the oars: a useful number, since although the river had been cleared of all shipping there was (typically enough) a fierce southwesterly gale, and progress upriver was difficult. Augustus Charles Pugin (father of the more famous A. W. Pugin) provided illustrations of the lying-in-state as well as the journey to St Paul's, and he painstakingly delineates the wind in the drapes, and the rough-crested waves on the water. A similarly black-draped flotilla – a mile long – followed Nelson's corpse towards the City of London, with guns firing in mournful salute.

So was it at this point that Greenwich became the place which, to Londoners, was the historical repository of everything maritime? The equivalent of Kensington Gore for all things musical, and Farnborough for aeronautics? After all, Nelson's connection with the place was slim: he had a friend at the Royal Naval Hospital. But it was a practicable waterfront place to start the obsequies, it was grand (that magnificent Painted Hall) and it was naval. Sailing ships found the reach along this southern shore the most convenient place to stop before London. (Steamships, which didn't care much about catching the wind – and consequently, about where they moored – were a long way off.) The Royal Dockyards were still busy. Many people in the

Greenwich area worked on the boats, or had some connection with them. Many officers in Nelson's fleet would have received an education at the academy begun in Greenwich by Thomas Weston, assistant Astronomer-Royal to the great John Flamsteed. The Royal Observatory was already responsible for the indispensable *Nautical Almanac*. The convergence of Greenwich and the deceased Nelson was irresistible. But it must have been a shock to the town – at the time with a population of 14,000 – to find twice that number besieging it every day for the three days of the public lying-in-state; just as it came as a shock, a few years later, when Greenwich became the site of one of London's more notorious fairs. Was this an intimation that the town was giving up a past that had made it important, and was turning into a place that was important only because it enshrined the past?

Jump forward to the founding of the National Maritime Museum in the 1930s, and that is exactly what seems to have happened. Greenwich, the place where naval officers did their book-learning, has officially turned into the repository of the nation's maritime memories. Hence the *Cutty Sark*. Following the interlude of the war – during which a stretch of the waterfront as well as the town centre were seriously damaged, and St Alfege's church was burnt out – the *Cutty Sark* arrived in Greenwich, towed into a specially built dry dock, in 1954. This was sited on the spot where the Ship Hotel – an impressive Victorian pile –

once stood. And the contrast between the old use of the site and its new one encapsulates the changes that Greenwich underwent throughout the nineteenth and twentieth centuries.

The Ship – unlike *Cutty Sark* – really was a piece of Greenwich history, having been through four separate incarnations since the sixteenth century. It had become notorious for the prices it charged for its whitebait and was a place where Dickens had wolfed down seafood. The Ship was, in its way, as important to Greenwich as the Oyster Bar in Grand Central Station is to New York, or Yates's Wine Lodge to Blackpool. The *Cutty Sark*, on the other hand, had nothing to do with Greenwich: built in Dumbarton in 1869, it had sailed across the world as a tea and wool clipper. But at least it was a ship. If it had anything to do with London, it was really to do with the docks across the river – it had berthed frequently at the East India Docks in Blackwall; but had also landed at Beachy Head, Hull and Deal. Nevertheless, when plans were being made to preserve it in the 1950s, Greenwich naturally suggested itself to the Cutty Sark Preservation Society – largely because of the presence of the Maritime Museum. The *Cutty Sark* was indeed offered as an exhibit; but the museum argued that it had nowhere to put it and no money to keep it in a reasonable state of repair. Undeterred, the Society found a sponsor in the form of the LCC, and the ship stayed put, even though a more natural resting place would have been among the wharves and sluices on the north side of the Thames.

So the Ship Hotel went, but the heritage theme remained – reinforced by the arrival, just over a decade later, of *Gipsy Moth IV*, the 54-foot ketch in which Sir Francis Chichester made the fastest round-the-world voyage in a small yacht, which was the longest passage by a small sailing vessel without a port of call. In order to break the latter record, Chichester had to fend off scurvy by growing mustard and cress in special trays on board ship. He finished his 226-day single-handed journey in Plymouth in May 1967, at the age of sixty-five ('Everything seems wrong about this voyage,' he wrote in his log at one stage. 'I hate it and I'm frightened'), and promptly sailed up the Thames to Greenwich. There, he was knighted by the queen on 13 June, in the middle of the Grand Square of the Royal Naval College. This was evidently a rather more decorous event than the one Drake would have taken part in, with a large, neat crowd seated on bleachers set up on the grass – the whole event done with a degree of careful modernity – but doing its best to enjoy the historical resonances it was trying to conjure up. Afterwards, *Gipsy Moth IV* (there were five *Gipsy Moths* altogether, one of them an aeroplane) was parked next to the *Cutty Sark*, its neat white shape (whiter than ever after a refit in 1996) looking positively toy-like in comparison with the enormous black bulk of the tea clipper. And so Greenwich's status as the keeper of our maritime heritage was confirmed.

So what happened to the rest of it? What became of all those hundreds of years of real activity, up and down the river? There are still wharves and jetties on the shoreline either side of central Greenwich, mainly prefabricated steel and composite structures, blank-faced and hidden behind security fences. And there are pleasure boats making their way down from Kew, at the Surrey end of the Thames, to tie up at Greenwich Pier on summer days. Elsewhere, there are scraps of the past which haven't yet vanished. Deptford Creek, for instance, working its way inland between factory buildings, has the occasional boat – a dredger, or a gravel container – lodged on its low-tide mud. And if you go across the creek and follow the road as it trails the northerly bend of the river, you eventually find yourself in the middle of the Pepys estate (having passed the site of Sayes Court without even knowing it), staring at the old entrance gateway to the Royal Victoria Victualling Yard in Grove Street. In the middle of acres of new-built housing, these beautiful stone-faced pillars, with a short row of impeccably proportioned and colonnaded yellow brick buildings behind, come as a complete shock. It was here that Red House biscuits were kept to feed the Navy; and at the gateway itself a permanent gas flame was kept alight for the yard's workers to light their cigarettes on – matches being banned in the yard, on account of the fire hazard.

Back in east Greenwich the nineteenth-century Enderby House sits in Ballast Quay, looking unimpressive but containing a neat little fragment of marine history in the form of its angled first-floor bay window – once used to command a view of ships moving along the river. Or what about the Woolwich Free Ferry, still solemnly plying its way across the river from north Woolwich to south Woolwich? Is it too fanciful to imagine it carrying a savour of the past, an echo from 1889, when the service was first instituted and paddle-steamers were the order of the day?

Two of the strangest relics of maritime Greenwich are not tucked away, but fully, bizarrely in view: and both are town halls. At least, Meridian House, in the High Road, was a town hall until the mid-1960s, when its functions were transferred to the Wellington Street Town Hall in Woolwich. But its scale and appearance still speak of an enormous civic self-belief, a strong sense of self-importance. Designed by Clifford Culpin, it draws its inspiration from Willem Dudok's brilliant Hilversum Town Hall – a De Stijl minor masterpiece. From its suave, geometric exterior to its zodiac mosaics over the front doorway, to its intricately detailed interiors, panelled in sycamore, teak, bird's-eye maple and cherrywood, furnished with satin curtains and tricked out with air conditioning and concealed heating, the Town Hall must have been a sensation when it opened in 1939. Its crowning glory – still there, unmissable from wherever you stand – is the tower, 165 feet high, and an act of homage from Culpin to Dudok. The tower is both a thing of wonder and a sign of lost greatness. Because why, after all, is it there?

The booklet which accompanied the opening of the Town Hall explains: 'The architects felt that, just as the spire of a

cathedral marks its position from the narrowest street of a medi-
aeval city, a tall tower to clearly indicate the position of the new
Town Hall should form an important unit in the architectural
conception.' As you make your way around Greenwich town,
you can put this claim to the test easily enough. It works. The
commemorative text then goes on, crucially, to note: 'At the
top, served by a lift, is a look-out room, with magnificent views
over the Thames, with all its teeming activity.' It also points out
that the room at the top of the tower is a small architectural
marvel in its own right, having a cantilever construction so that
its three glass walls are completely uninterrupted by intrusive
supporting masonry. What's more, the three clock dials that originally adorned the sides of the tower were once 'Illuminated with
blue-green fluorescent tubes', which must have made the building even more eerily powerful as soon as dusk began to fall. But
the fact is that it's not just a tower by means of which local
pedestrians can more easily spot the civic headquarters – it's a
tower which offers a stunning prospect of the Thames, 'with all
its teeming activity'. It looks like a harbour control centre or an
airport control tower because that's partly what it was intended
to be: a spot from which Greenwich could gaze down on the
commercial bustle of the river which meant so much to it and
which it clearly hoped would mean as much in the future as it
had in the past. It was a maritime statement, a gesture of kinship
with the open waters. And what happened to it? A mere two
decades after the end of the Second World War it lost its key

administrative place to a building down the road. Ten years later, and it was converted to offices, the old council chamber was partitioned, it became Meridian House, and at the time of writing it houses an independent tertiary college. A victim of circumstance and time.

And yet the other town hall struggles on, battling against ludicrous odds and the depredations of inner-city life – far worse, indeed, than those facing the old Greenwich Town Hall. The other town hall is the Deptford Town Hall, standing irrepressibly in the thunderous New Cross Road, with battalions of heavy lorries roaring past and the occasional passer-by stopping and staring in wonder at this extraordinary building in an otherwise forgotten part of town.

If Meridian House awes with its size and its intense modernity, then Deptford Town Hall (in the Borough of Lewisham) awes with its crazed inventiveness, its profusion of detail, its humour. Not many buildings can be said to be *funny*, but Deptford Town Hall is, and probably intentionally so. It was designed by the firm of Lanchester, Stewart and Rickards – Charles Rickards being the presiding genius behind this particular masterpiece – and it's worth toiling down Greenwich High Road to the point where it meets Deptford Bridge and Deptford Broadway, before carrying on into the New Cross Road, just to get that first shock of seeing this creation looming out over the pavements.

Not that it's especially tall – a mere three storeys plus lower ground – but its bulk, and the way this bulk is distributed, is wonderfully surprising. The lower portions of the façade (and this is what's chiefly interesting) are pretty well solemn classical pastiche, befitting the building's sober Edwardian completion date of 1905. But above that is a row of seafaring figures, marvellously carved statues (Drake and Nelson among them) gazing out disdainfully over the traffic, with, above the main door, billowing mythical winged figures with serpent tails. The doorway itself contains a huge iron lamp, a mixture of chains and seahorses and a pair of doors big enough for a medieval castle. As if this wasn't sufficient, the oriel window (embraced by two caryatids wearing fantastical helmets) above the main doorway is crested by the carved prow of a boat with banks of oars poking out of either side, which recedes grandly into a carven perspective. Above *that* is a substantial stone pediment, with a man-o'-war locked in a fierce sea battle (Trafalgar, perhaps?). And above *that*, hidden to some extent by the pediment and the roofline, but visible if you move a little to one side, is a clocktower with a railed lookout, a little belvedere gazing down on – what? The A2 trunk road as it squirms east towards Kent? Surely not to gaze at any passing ships, which – if they did exist – would be the best part of a mile away.

And yet the Town Hall is there, defiant, crazy, celebrating a confected nautical past with a half-serious, half-sent-up swagger. It's as if the National Maritime Museum had shrunk to a fifth of its present size, got riotously drunk and was elbowing itself down New Cross way, looking for a fight. The ships are gone, now. But of all the memorials to the great past in Greenwich, maybe this one, the least solemn, the least self-conscious, the least burdened with *gravitas*, is the best.

Or is that unfair to the Maritime Museum? Because, after a long period as one of London's more worthwhile-but-not-quite-essential museums (competing, after all, with the British Museum, the V & A, the Science and Natural History Museums, the Imperial War Museum, plus countless smaller collections in the centre of the city, plus all the art galleries, from National down) it has at last acquired some of the glamour it needs to keep itself in the first rank.

This has come about as the result of the new building programme, which has transformed the way it looks, and the way it displays its exhibits. Nowadays it has an immense and potentially daunting collection, one so big that it *needs* a decent display. Not only does the museum have all the items it was endowed with back in the 1930s, but it's also been endowed with many more recently – in total, some 2,500 ship models, 4,000 paintings, 50,000 charts, and countless unusual and irreplacable pieces. These range from a sixteenth-century ivory mariner's compass to a bust of Lord Fisher by Jacob Epstein, to a ship's biscuit, to a 1906 marine compound engine, to the whole of *Suhaili* – the 32-foot ketch in which yachtsman Robin Knox-Johnston sailed in the world's first solo non-stop circumnavigation of the globe in 1969. And all these things have to have somewhere big and dynamic and modern in which to be housed – somewhere the museum may at last have created with its Neptune Court Project. This has transformed the place from something a little bit dowdy, a little bit gloomy, with its High Victorian north façade and its stodgy wings, to something bright, lively, intriguing. The covering over of the central courtyard is a real stroke of genius. The biggest single-span glazed roof in Europe, this brilliant fusion of interior and exterior eats up a large part of the £20 million budget – but is without a doubt worth it, as it brings coherence, light, an entirely new ambience to the museum, and so lifts the exhibits immeasurably. New galleries and new themes are also important – shipbuilding, navigation, warships, cargoes – but as a potent symbol of regeneration, the Neptune Court Project is at the heart of it all. The view of the National Maritime Museum from the Romney Road used to be one of London's more dispiriting sights. Now, it looks genuinely exciting: and that excitement informs the whole institution. Maybe *this* is the answer to the question of Greenwich and the burden of its maritime tradition: money, style and confidence.

WORKING

I F YOU WANT to get back to the days of hard times on the river, if you want to catch a sense of being in the crowd shuffling towards a long day's toil, then try walking through the Greenwich Foot Tunnel on a busy morning. It can be uncanny: the voices echoing off the glazed tiled walls, the stuffiness, the clattering of shoes on the cold floor, the narrowness of the tunnel (a mere 11 feet in diameter), the oppressive sense of the Thames just above your head, the fact that the floor slopes downwards to the mid-point before climbing up again, so that you always reach the other end in a state of mild, plodding exertion – all these things conspire to generate a feeling of being part of a large, tired, shambling mass, heading blindly from one side of the water to the other.

This progress, south to north and back again, has been going since at least the sixteenth century – and probably earlier. Of course, there was no tunnel, then; and the ferry service was naturally prone to the problems which affect all boats on a tidal river. Pepys refers to a not untypical problem involving himself and Sir George and Lady Carteret – Naval Treasurer Sir George Carteret, whose official residence was situated in Deptford. The three of them, having crossed the river by ferry, had to endure an irksome delay while they waited for their coach to be transported across after them, the tide being temporarily too low for the ferry to land: 'So we were fain to stay in the unlucky Isle of Doggs, in a chill place, the morning cool, and wind fresh, above two, if not three hours, to our great discontent.' But by 1676 a more reliable ferry service was regularly transporting workers from the Greenwich side to the north side, where the docks provided a more or less constant source of work. As time passed, so the numbers of dock workers increased, and the rowed ferryboat was replaced by a steamboat. But the amount of traffic coursing up and down the river had also increased, and by the end of the nineteenth century – the Empire's apogee – the little ferry steamboat was starting to become a hazard on one of the busiest parts of the Thames.

The answer was clearly to build a tunnel (another Tower Bridge – recently opened in 1894, and the marvel of its day – would have been out of the question). In 1899 Cochrane & Sons were given the job of building the new tunnel for the London County Council, and in 1902 it was formally opened. Workers could freely foot-commute from the south side to Cubitt Town, as the development on the Isle of Dogs was now known. (This had been started by the builder William Cubitt during the 1840s to provide housing and other services for men working in and around the docks; eventually it gave its name to the whole eastern end of the Isle of Dogs peninsula, which is still known as Cubitt Town, despite the gradual encroachments of end-of-the century Docklands developments.) Against the novel convenience of the tunnel, however, was the fact that there are 100 steps from ground level down to the tunnel floor on the Greenwich side, and 88 steps on the Isle of Dogs side; quickly it became clear that lifts were needed at either end. These duly began operation in 1904, and since then almost nothing about the tunnel has changed.

Most of the 200,000 tiles on the walls are the same ones that were put in a hundred years ago; the length – just under a quarter of a mile – hasn't altered; the depth of water, 53 feet of it at high tide, is just the same: seeping at points through the cast-iron tunnel segments it emerges in obscure scale deposits on the inner face. Even the lifts are the same – or at least, look the same. In fact, the old lift mechanisms were replaced with new ones in 1992; but the boroughs of Greenwich and Tower Hamlets, which jointly funded the improvements, decided to keep the wood panelling from the 1904 versions and install them in the new lifts. Which only adds to the sense of stepping back in time as you board the lift car, an attendant sitting silently in one corner to operate the doors (and a similar attendant on the other side, sitting in an almost identical lift car, making you wonder sometimes which side of the river you're actually on and which side you meant to cross to), and descend to the lower depths. (For real enthusiasts, there's another foot tunnel very like it, a little further down at Woolwich. Opened in 1912 and serving the same purpose, it imparts something of the same melancholy sense of transport back through time.) The glass-domed roofs of the circular entrance buildings on either side of the Greenwich Tunnel look curiously misplaced – do they let light into a race of Morlocks below? Or shine up like a pair of car headlights into the night sky? The dome on the south side, in Cutty Sark Gardens, looks especially bizarre, isolated as it is in a lake of post-war concrete.

But it symbolises something important about the area – the fact that although Greenwich town itself is a remarkable assemblage of history, science and architecture (added to UNESCO's World Heritage List in 1997, and now keeping company with the Grand Canyon, the Taj Mahal and the Great Wall of China), and has a relatively refined surface appearance (quite apart from all the obviously memorable big buildings, it has a great deal of Georgian and Regency architecture, with few Victorian lumpen developments to spoil the trend), it is nonetheless a place where people have had to make a living. Indeed, nearby Deptford, Charlton, Woolwich, Lewisham and Plumstead have often found the going pretty tough.

And when you read that a census of 1841 found that the majority of those Greenwich inhabitants living at the Church Street end of town were still connected by some sort of trade to the water – either directly on the river, or at sea – it's tempting to combine that knowledge with the Greenwich heritage, and imagine the place as a kind of inland Regency Brighton, or a Henley-on-Thames on the estuary: genteel, pleasure-seeking, frivolous. However, T. L. Brooker's photographic portraits of Greenwich, taken at the turn of the century, show that the real world, especially down by the river's edge, was not that sweet. Brewhouse Lane, for instance, was a short, grimy passage running parallel with the river, bounded by Huntley's coal yard (whose overhead railway line ran across the top of the lane) and with a mysterious drinking establishment called Fubbs Yacht halfway down. At one end of Brewhouse Lane was Dark Entry, captured by Brooker in a grim, industrial monotone, before he moves down to the lane proper, with its peeling walls, scratched grafitti in the plaster, soot, walls crowned by broken glass, and one or two hesitant locals peering out of the shadows. Church Street, leading down to the flight of steps that was once the main landing place for boats from London and Kent, is shown with Brewhouse Lane emerging on the left of the picture, a knot of urchins sitting on the steps to the right, grafitti on the dingy walls in the foreground, and a sense of overhanging gloom and decay. Just round the corner, the Sugar Loaf beerhouse in Billingsgate Street has attracted a group of men from Huntley's.

Standing outside, they wait for it to open. The atmosphere of shabby indolence (one full coal wagon drawn up outside; several more standing around empty) is reinforced by the state of the pub itself. The Sugar Loaf (with the word GIN prominent on its outer wall) is not only dark, neglected and covered in filth, but has also lost its sign – apparently along with its self-respect.

Scenes like this would have been mirrored all along the waterfront, with its wharves, boatyards and watermen, and out through the surrounding towns. Nichol's grime-covered lime-burners toiled away in the Woolwich Road, Charlton, operating a pair of smoking, fiercely heated bottle kilns. At the Cemetery Brickfield in Plumstead (which abutted the Woolwich Cemetery) gangs of men dug the local clay, chalk and brick earth, and fired the bricks. John Penn and Sons was a thriving marine engine manufactory based in the Blackheath Road; the Associated Motor Cycles works in Plumstead was getting ready to become one of the biggest motorcycle manufacturers in the world, starting with push-bikes in the nineteenth century, producing the first 'Matchless' motorcycle in 1899 and reaching a peak of production during the 1950s. Wheen's Soap Works in Deptford rendered down animal fat from the cattle market opened on the site of the old dockyards in 1871 and may well have used in their works a steam engine retrieved from the break-up of the *Great Eastern* – Brunel's huge, 32,000-ton steamship, built just across the river at Millwall in 1857. The Siemens factory at Woolwich turned out electrical machinery and components; and there was the huge Royal Arsenal at Woolwich – employing 70,000 people at its peak during the First World War, enclosing three miles of Plumstead Marshes, enjoying its own internal railway system, and responsible for a succession of disastrous explosions which killed several people and caused damage for miles around.

Back on the waterfront were the gasworks owned by the South Metropolitan Gas Company and sited on the Blackwall peninsula – the finger of land to the east of Greenwich, poking back towards the Isle of Dogs. These were opened in 1886 and soon became the largest works in Europe: a major industrial enterprise a scant mile from the doors of the Queen's House. At around the same time, Billingsgate Dock, near where *Gipsy Moth IV* is now dry-docked, would have been crowded with fishing smacks. Following its widening and improvement in 1850, Billingsgate was the principal Dock in Greenwich and the home of the local fishing industry: hard to conceive of now, but in the mid-nineteenth century fishermen would set sail from the Greenwich shore at Eastertime, sail as far as Iceland and the Faeroes, and come back at the end of summer with their catches. This was no more than the continuation of a tradition which had been going on for centuries, and which was central to Greenwich's concept of itself. But as Billingsgate Dock was being fitted out for the second half of the century, Grimsby in Lincolnshire was also setting itself up for the fishing trade – and being a good 200 miles nearer the fishing grounds, was starting to prove irresistibly attractive as a base from which to operate. The Greenwich fishermen moved north, and so, by the turn of the century, had the whole of Greenwich's fishing industry.

So there were always light-industrial concerns, marine businesses, large-scale factories, hard up against Greenwich's relative gentility. One of London's least-used but most obscurely rewarding walks ('The best Thames-side walk in London,' says Nairn, overstating his case a little) runs along the river from the Cutty Sark Gardens along the Five Foot Walk (the footpath in front of the Royal Naval College, ceded to the public in 1731) and all the way to the Blackwall Tunnel. If you take this walk, you find that it hints at the commercial life that once was – albeit it in a drear, funereal way, given the stretches of desolation, and the fact that for much of the time the footpath is bleakly under-used by pedestrians.

Clearly the first big enterprise, once you pass the Trafalgar Tavern and the Trinity Hospital almshouses dating from 1613 (but with an 1812 Gothick building), is the old LCC power station. Originally a relatively modest stables for the old turn-of-the-century horse-drawn trams, the site was taken over by the London County Council when it assumed responsibility for London's tram system. It promptly built this colossal generating station (at a time when electricity was still principally used in public and commercial enterprises, and not in the home), utterly changing the character of the shoreline. At first powered by coal, it was later converted to gas and oil, and had a set of jet-engine-powered gas turbine generators put in during the 1960s. At the time of writing, it uses mostly natural gas to perform its function as a back-up to the main London Underground generators in Chelsea – which is why the enormous, morbid fuel jetty sticking out into the river is so provocative. Once colliers tied up along-side it to deliver coal and take away the residual ashes; deliveries of oil came the same way. But now it does nothing, except look terrifying and gargantuan and sinister – one clear reason why the Poet Laureate, C. Day Lewis (a resident of nearby Croom's Hill) set a murder mystery there when writing thrillers under the pseudonym Nicholas Blake.

After that, you find yourself wandering through Ballast Quay – the spot where ships were loaded up with gravel ballast dug out on Blackheath and carted down Maze Hill. Deposited in their holds, this gave them stability on their empty journeys back to their home ports. No sign of anything much now, except for the Old Harbour Master's House of 1854, the revamped Cutty Sark pub, and some newly built houses done in a faint echo of the old clapboard timber homes of Church Street. And then you're really into that semi-dereliction which hints at the active past of Greenwich, in the form of Lovell's Wharf – ruined cranes and deserted buildings – followed by the mysterious vanishing trick which is Enderby's Wharf.

This was once the site of a ropewalk run by the three Enderby brothers – who, incidentally, pioneered Antarctic whaling and whose employee, John Biscoe, discovered in 1831 a mountainous region rising out of Antarctica, loyally naming it Enderby Land in tribute to his bosses. When the whaling moved on, Enderby's became a cable factory (the Telegraph Construction and Maintenance Co., incorporating, exotically, the Gutta Percha Co.), which used to pay out steel hawsers and electric cables on a cradle of wires, straight on to the cable ships moored several yards out in the river. It even provided the electric cable which the *Great Eastern* used to complete the first successful trans-atlantic telegraph link in 1866. One of the buildings which remains from this time – a small, white affair, nothing grand, adjoining the angular Enderby House – has gutta-percha leaves decorating its face, in recognition of the fact that gutta-percha was, for a long time, the insulating material which covered the cables. Standard Telephones picked up the site in 1970, and the last submarine cable was manufactured and loaded on to ships in 1979. Now there is this little group of shorefront buildings, new offices where the factory once stood, and, like a fantastical mon ument to the past, the broken remains of the machinery once used to pay out the cabling. A squat, massive steel gantry stands four square, facing the river, and, just beyond it, a heavy-duty steel wheel with the remains of a complex braking and feeding system attached to it: the dinosaur bones of what was once a nationally renowned – and *internationally* renowned – industry. And when you turn round from these gloomy relics, you see a gap in the buildings, still there for the cabling to run through – a gap which leads straight back to nothing; only a car park and an anonymous business centre. Enderby's has disappeared.

From there, you move into a still-operating industrial zone, with a refinery, heaps of aggregate and building materials, and a sprawling chemical works, interspersed with odd bits of river-front dereliction. And at the end, looming larger and larger with every step, is the Millennium Dome. So you stop, turn and look back across the river. The view is spectacular and strange: the murky, grey Thames doing its best to reflect the new houses built on the north bank, and the long, untidy line of Greenwich's industrial inheritance, straggling down to the power station, the almshouses and, like something from another world altogether, the palely gleaming columns and pediments of the Royal Naval College. One look sums it up: prettiness and gentility have not been a option at Greenwich for generations. It has always had to compromise between refinement and roughness. Indeed, one impressive photographic panorama, taken in 1879 from the top of Observatory Hill, shows the Royal Naval College and the Queen's House elegantly spread out across the right foreground, framed by full-leafed summer trees; while off to either side and disappearing into a smog-filled distance stretch miles and miles of smoking factory chimneys and the crude, uncompromising shapes of the buildings they service. It's the scene Sir John Liddell was trying to conjure up in his rant about 'the daily increase of houses and manufactories . . . the injurious influence of air vitiated by the clouds of dense black smoke and impurities . . . from the chimney tops of steamers and manufactories that are gathering around it'. It is the constant relationship between well-to-do, elegant Greenwich and the gritty hardworking real world around it.

So there you had the hard-working people of Greenwich. But what about the hard-working people of the rest of London, who were beginning to make their way in growing numbers downriver to Greenwich Park, to escape some of London's noise and smoke?

This had been open to the public since the eighteenth century, and had rapidly become a focal point for working Londoners at play. Samuel Johnson had lodgings in Greenwich in 1737 (in Church Street; quite possibly in a row of weatherboarded houses which were still standing in the nineteenth century, when T. L. Brooker photographed them), and took advantage of the park's recent opening to spend a good deal of time there, completing *Irene* (a tragedy – 'Angelic Greatness is Angelic Virtue') and writing *London* – in which the lines appear:

> On *Thames*'s banks, in silent thought we stood,
> Where Greenwich smiles upon the silver Flood:
> Struck with the Seat that gave Eliza birth,
> We kneel, and kiss the consecrated Earth.

Years later, in 1763, after Johnson had moved upriver into the city, he and Boswell found themselves in Greenwich Park on a day trip. Boswell read the 'Greenwich smiles' passage from *London* and asked the great man if he still thought the park an appealing spot. Johnson replied, 'Yes, sir; but not equal to Fleet Street'. (He also remarked that the Royal Naval Hospital – apart from being too much detached – was 'Too magnificent for a place of charity', anticipating Nathaniel Hawthorne by a hundred years.)

Nevertheless, it was Greenwich Park, rather than Fleet Street, which became one of London's chief centres of leisure and repose. And as the nineteenth century progressed, the park's popularity increased, because of improved communications – by river, down to the new Greenwich Pier, built in 1836; and by rail, once the London–Greenwich line was opened in 1838. Indeed, to improve its amenities, the park very nearly acquired what would have been one of the most terrifying monuments in London: the neoclassical artist John Flaxman (most famous for his Wedgwood pottery designs) planned a huge statue of Britannia to stand on top of Greenwich Hill commemorating British naval victories in the Napoleonic Wars. A bit like a British Statue of Liberty, it would have been more than 220 feet tall. (Nelson's Column comes in at a mere 185 feet in total.) Fortunately, the idea was squashed, not least because this monster would have completely dominated the Naval Hospital below.

What *did* happen around this time was the gradual establishment of the two notorious Greenwich fairs: one at Easter, one at Whitsun. These events became so infamous that they attracted the attention of writers such as Thackeray (who, in his *Sketches and Travels in London*, mentions the 'Questionable company' associated with the fairs) and Dickens – who was, by way of contrast, a fan of Greenwich and used it more than once in his writing. Dickensians are quick to point out, *inter alia*, that at one stage in *David Copperfield* our hero 'Gave up the pursuit of the young man with the donkey-cart and started for Greenwich . . .'; while in *Our Mutual Friend* there are extensive goings-on in Greenwich when Pa takes Bella Wilfer for a meal by the river; followed, much later, by the great Wilfer–Rokesmith riverside marriage banquet.

As for the fair – this gets a lengthy dissection in *Sketches by Boz*, of 1836–37. Here Dickens adopts a favourite posture of wide-eyed yet tolerant amusement, patrolling the crowds and drawing our attention to the profusion of snacks and treats available from the stallholders – pickled salmon (with fennel), 'Oysters, with shells as large as cheese-plates', and 'divers specimens of snail . . . floating in a somewhat bilious-looking green liquid' – as a foretaste of the reckless consumption characteristic of the rest of the event. He also makes great play of one practice: young men would 'drag young ladies up the steep hill which leads to the Observatory, and then drag them down again, at the very top of their speed, greatly to the derangement of their curls and bonnet-caps and much to the edification of the lookers-on below'.

This custom had in fact been going on in one form or another since the early eighteenth century, and was known as 'Tumbling' – originally it was no more than a frenzied race down the hill in Greenwich Park known as the Giant's Steps; or, for the more reckless, down the steeper hill under the terrace of the Royal Observatory. As time went by, however, the racing became more chaotic and more dangerous. The *Daily Journal* of 1730 contains a report of a young woman breaking her neck at Tumbling, while another apparently broke her leg and a third fractured her skull against a tree. By the 1820s this had evolved into something close to the free-for-all Dickens writes about: a contemporary account explains that 'In rows the men and girls lined up across the Park and arm-in-arm ran down the slope: some kept their feet, some rolled to the bottom'. Dickens, not wishing to spoil the mood, steers clear of the problems of injuries and breakages, before turning his attention to the 'scratcher': a little hand-held gadget described by its promoters as 'A devastating and ingenious piece of mechanism' which was rolled down the middle of the victim's back so that it made a noise 'resembling the laceration of a garment'. As a gesture to good taste, he completes the scene by drawing a romantic comparison between the park by moonlight and the artificially lit fair entertainments after dark.

But what principally animates him is the mob itself. 'Imagine yourself,' he says, 'in an extremely dense crowd, which swings you to and fro, and in and out, and every way but the right one; add to this the screams of women, the shouts of boys, the clanging of gongs, the firing of pistols, the ringing of bells, the bellowings of speaking-trumpets, the squeaking of penny-dittoes, the noise of a dozen bands with three drums in each, all playing different tunes at the same time, the hallooing of showmen and an occasional roar from the wildbeast shows; and you are in the very centre and heart of the fair.' This really was the essence of the thing – the seething mass of revellers who descended on Greenwich at holiday time, in search of release from their workaday city lives. At its height in the late 1830s and '40s, the arrival of Greenwich Fair meant that a fleet of fifty steamers would be commandeered to bring the crowds to and from London, unloading as many as 150,000 people a day. And what had they come for? Apart from dragging each other up and down hill, eating and drinking, gazing at the illuminations, shouting, whistling, singing, letting off pistols and attacking one another with 'scratchers', the common folk of London had come to see John Richardson's celebrated booth.

Richardson was one of London's most famous itinerant showmen, an impresario who at one stage had Edmund Kean (the great tragedian, philanderer and drunk) in his troupe, and who was renowned for giving amazing value for money. For the mob at the Greenwich Fair, he would live up to his reputation by staging an overture, followed by a melodrama containing no less than three murders and a ghost, followed by a pantomime, and ending with a comic song. The whole spectacle, crammed on to one portable (and therefore tiny) stage, would take no more than twenty minutes from end to end. The audience would then depart, satiated, and the stage would be cleared for the next performance, following on a few minutes later.

Competition for Richardson's crown could be fierce, though. Algar's Crown and Anchor Dancing Booth was probably the first dance hall open to the general public (admission one shilling), and was likewise a regular feature of the fairs. Two dance areas – capable of holding 2,000 people in total – were erected in a marquee, while food and drink were served in a third space. Dickens was particularly taken with Algar's offering: 'Immediately on your right hand,' he writes, 'as you enter, after paying your money, is a refreshment place, at which cold beef, roast and boiled, French rolls, stout, wine, tongue, ham, even fowls . . . are displayed in tempting array.' But that was just a taster, something to amuse the appetite. The serious stuff was taking place on the dance floor, where, according to Dickens, 'the dust is blinding, the heat insupportable', and where 'the dancing, itself, beggars description – every figure lasts about an hour, and the ladies bounce up and down in the middle, with a degree of spirit which is quite indescribable'.

The only thing that might have torn Algar's revellers away from this pandemonium would have been George Wombwell's wild animal acts – 'the wildbeast shows'. The locals greeted Wombwell's Menagerie with real alarm, as it was generally believed that he employed a man for the express purpose of snatching pet cats and dogs in the dead of night, to feed to his touring lions and tigers. Not that this bothered the crowds: the show was all, especially as one year the Lion Queen (the daughter of one of the musicians) was mauled to death in front of the audience, and the chance to see tragedy repeat itself was probably too strong for many to resist.

The whole spectacle is nothing more than the unadulterated sight of London's working classes – Dickens's 'clerks and 'prentices' – having a good time, and it caused him to coin a description which stuck to the fair like a burr. 'A periodical breaking out we suppose a sort of spring rash,' was the indelible description, 'a 3-day fever which cools the blood for 6 months afterwards, and at the expiration of which London is restored to its old habits of plodding industry.' But naturally it caused the more refined inhabitants of Greenwich an inordinate amount of distress. They started to make official complaints about the fair as early as 1825, when a parish petition was got together, bemoaning the fact that 'The numbers of the profligate part of the lower orders have been increased'. This went on to note that 'A very great addition is made to this evil by the open and powerful incentives to licentiousness', rounding off with the cry that the fair's depraved goings-on offended 'against the best feelings of Christian morality'. This, unfortunately, had no immediate effect, and the fairs continued, enraging the local community and scandalising the pious. Another attempt to stamp out the revelry came in 1857, when 2,000 people formally protested to the Commissioner of Police. This time there was clearly too great a body of opinion to ignore, and the Commissioner issued an order – not against the stallholders and itinerants of the fair itself, but against the landowners who had let spaces for the various booths and stalls. There was no appeal. The fairs came to an end.

At least, they did in Greenwich. But Blackheath was just up the hill, and was in some ways even more suited to reckless pleasure.

Now, Blackheath, eliding seamlessly into Greenwich via the park, has a slightly odd relationship with it – something like that of a slightly suaver younger brother, or junior partner, with his superior – even though it, too, sits by the same Roman road to Canterbury, and was the spot on which the Danes were camped while they held the wretched St Alphege captive in the eleventh century. Indeed, it has a history which stretches back almost as far as that of its more illustrious neighbour. The fact is, though, that Blackheath was for a long time less the salubrious village it is now, and more a large open space with a reputation. The table of land which is the Heath, and across which the A2 now rolls, is still a dauntingly broad expanse: as you come up upon it from the centre of the village it seems almost limitless, sloping away at its edges into an invisible hinterland. Even with the constant rumble of traffic heading east–west, it can sometimes assume the look of a chunk of open moorland dropped into a London suburb – like the empty, barren waste which Shakespeare briefly employs in *Henry VI, Part 2*, when the Irish rebel, Jack Cade, meets Sir Humphrey and William Stafford on Blackheath and kills them both ('The bodies shall be dragged at my horse's heels, till I do come to London, where we will have the Mayor's sword borne before us').

Which is why things tended to happen there that took advantage of its size and openness. Wat Tyler assembled his followers on Blackheath in 1381 at the start of the Peasants' Revolt; Henry VII fought his battle with Michael Joseph and his band of Cornish rebels on Blackheath in 1497 (a group of men building a barn at Greenwich Palace supposedly dropped their tools and ran up the hill to watch the fight); Henry VIII accepted Anne of Cleves there, after the embarrassment of their first meeting in Rochester; John Wesley used it for revivalist meetings; the first golf club in England was allegedly founded here in 1608, a fact commemorated in the name given to Goffers Road (although according to the *Chronicles of Blackheath Golfers*, the club really started in 1787); the Blackheath Football Club really is the oldest open Rugby Union club in the world; and Blackheath, being broad, open, full of travellers and hard to police, was famous for many years for its highwaymen.

In the eighteenth century, its principal hold on the public imagination was precisely as a den of thieves and robbers (Dickens – again – makes fleeting use of Blackheath's more sinister qualities in *A Tale of Two Cities*), a belief which was pretty well founded in fact. A typical newspaper report of 1742 reads: 'A gentleman was stopped near the sixmile stone on Blackheath by a man on foot, who had something over his face. He drew a pistol from under his coat, and desired the gentleman would let him have some money, who gave him 5s., saying he could spare no more. He asked the gentleman's pardon, and said he was drove to this through the treacherous and cruel usage he met from a near relation who reduced him to this extremity.' Ten years later, and the scourge is still there. 'Last Thursday afternoon between five and six,' begins a newspaper report from 1752, 'a young gentleman was robbed in the Woolwich stage-coach by two highwaymen, genteelly mounted, near the Artichoke on Blackheath. They both came up to the coach-door; one of them clapped a pistol to his breast and demanded his money, on which he delivered all he had, but desired they would return him one shilling to pay his coach hire, which they refused, but otherwise behaved very complaisantly, shook hands with him and wished him good-night.' Nearly a decade on, and the robbers are still busy – but the victim is less well treated: from a report of September 1761 – 'A man coming from Greenwich to Leadenhall Market was stopt by two footpads a little way from his house, who took from him nine guineas, then carried him into an adjacent field, tied his hands and feet, and so left him; his horse being let loose returned home, which caused some persons to be sent in quest, who found him by hearing him moan . . .'

Just three instances out of many – so many, in fact, that the more law-abiding inhabitants of Blackheath clubbed together in 1753 to establish a fund which would help to suppress this chronic lawlessness. They offered rewards such as: 'For the conviction . . . of any one breaking into the house of a subscriber, £15'; and for the conviction of 'Every one guilty of stealing their poultry, fish, linens, lead, or iron gates, £2.' Hard to imagine now, in modern Blackheath, but this was what the place was reduced to, two hundred and fifty years ago.

This ill reputation was still clinging to the Heath in 1871, when it became the site of one of Greenwich's most notorious crimes. In the dead of night, a young woman was discovered crawling around the edge of the Heath with a terrible wound in her head, apparently the result of a series of vicious hammer blows. She died in Guy's Hospital, the victim of a murder so ghastly that by the following Sunday 20,000 people were reported to have crowded on to Blackheath to visit the spot where she had been found. When it became known that the murderer was in all likelihood a well-to-do young man called Edmund Pook, living in Greenwich, just across the road from St Alfege's, things became even more emotionally charged. Now it was not just murder, but class conflict: the girl had been employed as a servant by the young man's family, was made pregnant by him, was then sacked by his mother and had clearly been done away with to conceal the family's shame. Pook himself had not only been seen hurrying along the outskirts of Blackheath at the time of the murder, but had also enquired about buying a hammer in Deptford, *and* had been found to have bloodstains on his clothes – and yet, amazingly enough, was acquitted at his trial. This led to a near-riot as a mob descended on the Pooks' house, demanding justice. Furiously denunciatory pamphlets were sold in the streets and a truck drove through the centre of town with a tableau vivant on the back, showing a young woman being hammered to death by a depraved-looking man. Pook, however, was never convicted . . .

But these alarms and panics eventually passed. Blackheath village grew and the trains came, and the prevailing tone changed from slightly frontier-town lawlessness to bourgeois tranquillity. And it became clear that the Heath itself, no longer haunted by villains, would suit a fair perfectly. So the showmen and hucksters and stallholders who had recently been evicted from Greenwich decamped a mile or so further south, and carried on much as before. Everyone went to the same shows as they had in the past (although there was no opportunity for ritual hair-dragging, as there had been in Greenwich Park), everyone misbehaved in the time-honoured fashion and, equally predictably, the authorities decided they had had enough and declared the fair illegal in 1868. Did this piece of official interference deter the crowds? Not a bit. The following year, 50,000 people turned up on the off-chance of something happening – and there were the showmen and stallholders, waiting for them as before. The fair went off as usual, after an extremely small police presence failed to make any impression on the people's will. A bit later on, the Metropolitan Board of Works tried to take away some of the fair's appeal by reducing the number of licences issued to stallholders, but the fair went on ... and on ... and as the nineteenth century turned into the twentieth, people were still turning up for the ever-popular donkey rides, the swings and sideshows: the common man, in search of escape. By the 1920s the fair had been moved to an old gravel pit, and contemporary pictures show gondola swings, a helter-skelter, and groups of people crunching their way through acres of harsh light aggregate. As time progressed the fairs became – like any travelling fair – less eccentric, more standardised, more the conventional mix of bumper car rides and penny sideshows. And when the fair wasn't on, the circus would call round; until the present, when the Blackheath Fair rolls round with impeturbable regularity, everyone has a good time, and almost no one summons to mind the 'periodical breaking out', or the 'three-day fever' of those early years in the Greenwich Park. Only the ghost of the event remains.

WEALTHY

I F THE Greenwich Fair moved to Blackheath, it was because the Heath was immediately next door, it was broad, it continued the tradition of the fairs by another means. But at first sight, the difference in atmosphere for the fair-goers must have been marked. Greenwich Park is a neat rectangle, bounded by walls and gates, and with a clear and tidy topography. It rises in the south on a series of gentle hills (Croom's Hill running along the western side, Maze Hill on the east), with the Royal Observatory acting as a focal point, before falling away to the flat riverside, on which the great Naval College is immemorially framed. It is a definite park, with its avenues of trees (still with something French about their arrangement, no matter what Le Nôtre's involvement may or may not have been), its formal paths and its scattered buildings. When you walk around it, you stroll, as if it still was a very large back garden to a great house. It is, in its way, domestic.

Blackheath, on the other hand, is a confused jigsaw of triangular patches of grassland, divided by roads of all sizes and categories, and appearing to enjoy no internal consistency at all. It is almost treeless, permanently windy, and – thanks to its relative height (150 feet above sea level) and its slightly domed shape – is a place with a huge sky: something normally impossible to find in Greater London. The only building to make a real impact on the Heath is a Victorian church, All Saints (designed by Benjamin Ferrey in 1859), which sits uncomfortably on the edge, its spire pointing dourly heavenwards. A hundred years ago, the Heath would have looked even more intimidating, covered as it was with outcrops of gorse and scatterings of old gravel pits, the last of which were being quarried as late as 1869 (Maryon Park, a little further east in Charlton, was opened in 1890, the product of landscaping a whole warren of similar disused chalk and gravel pits) It wasn't until 1946 that the Heath was smoothly grassed over, and given a slightly more benign appearance. Nevertheless, when you cross Blackheath on foot, you don't stroll: you walk briskly. You might also infer from Blackheath that Blackheath Village itself would be a slightly wild place, very much on the edge of things – especially if you compare the Heath with, say Hampstead Heath in north London, or Richmond Park – both of which also have open, windblown stretches (Richmond in particular), but neither of which seems anything but wholly middle-class and tamed.

The irony is that while Greenwich Park is more civilised, more bourgeois than Blackheath, the opposite is true of Blackheath Village and Greenwich Town. Greenwich Town has had too many years of economic ups and downs to be anything other than a complete mixture of tastes, backgrounds and incomes. Blackheath Village is affluent, and wears its affluence with pride. As *Burrough's Pocket Guide* put it, back in 1909, 'The Village has a cheerful bustling appearance; while yet retaining just a soupçon of ruralness that appeals so gratefully to the senses'. It sounds a little smug, and in a way, Blackheath Village still is.

Until the 1700s there was almost no village to speak of. No matter what historical incidents took place on the Heath, and no matter how many stagecoaches had to make their perilous way down Shooters Hill Road, the Village remained no more than a handful of cottages, two public houses and no church. It was only in the eighteenth century, with the building of Michael Searles's Paragon development (begun in 1792), that Blackheath started to put on weight. As London grew, so the Village – near enough to be within reach, far away enough to be out of the crowds – suddenly became a popular spot for the rising well-to-do middle classes. At the same time, John Cator, a wealthy timber merchant from nearby Beckenham, established the great Cator

Aerial view of Greenwich c.1934

View across the Thames of the Royal Naval College c.1900

St Alfege's Church, Greenwich c.1890s

King Charles', King William's and Queen Mary's Buildings, Royal Naval College c.1887

The Painted Hall, Royal Naval College 1865

Henry VIII, Thomas Howard
Duke of Norfolk, Charles
Brandon Duke of Suffolk,
Anne Boleyn, Mary Tudor
Dowager Queen of France,
and Margaret Dowager Queen
of Scotland enjoy a dance in a
meadow with Greenwich
Palace in the background
c.1535

Charlton House, Greenwich in 1845

The Tulip Staircase in the Queen's House, Greenwich

Deptford Creek

Deptford Town Hall in 1977. The windows are being boarded up to avoid damage from a potentially violent National Front rally the next day

A steamboat excursion to Greenwich on the Thames on an Easter Monday. Illustrated London News 1847

The Royal Observatory at Greenwich c.1908

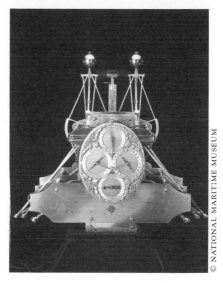

John Harrison's Chronometer H1

The Great Equatorial Telescope at the
Royal Observatory c.1908

Industrial site at East Greenwich

The Millennium Dome

Estate (and funded the Paragon) and drove the area's development on with a programme of speculative building. By the first
quarter of the nineteenth century the Village was immensely
larger, and when the railway came in 1849, Blackheath's position
as a favoured outer London suburb was guaranteed. The only
minor deviation from this steady progression came when the
Blackheath Cavern was rediscovered in 1780. This was a system
of several caves and a well, which could have been (and could
still be) anything from prehistoric (and possibly sacrificial) in
origin, to mere chalk pits, excavated in the fifteenth century
and since forgotten. Whatever their origins, they were a source of
wonder for both locals and tourists and remained so for decades.
So popular an attraction were they that in 1850 an entrepreneur
called J. Sleaman organised something he called *Un Grand Bal
Masqué*, which he held in the Blackheath Cavern itself. He
charged one shilling a head admission, and claimed that the
music sounded 'truly wonderful two hundred and eighty feet
below the ground'. So successful was Mr Sleaman's enterprise
that other balls followed, until the fateful year of 1853, when the
final masked ball disintegrated in chaos after pranksters either –
depending on which account you read – stank the place out with
asafoetida or plunged it into pitch blackness by simultaneously
putting out all the candles. Either way, the event ended in panic
and confusion and the Cavern was closed up – only reopening
briefly in 1946, to allow an official inspection to be carried out.
When the inspection team went down, they found mementoes

from the last ball still scattered around, left behind in the hysteria nearly a hundred years earlier.

But if the caves, the masked balls, and, indeed, the annual fairs were a blot on the landscape, everything else went very nicely for Blackheath. You can see just how nicely things turned out when you walk around there today. Leaving the railway station (with its iron notice plate by the entrance – THIS BRIDGE IS INSUFFICIENT TO CARRY A HEAVY MOTOR CAR) you find yourself in a snug little valley of shops and houses. The actual centre of the Village is in a dip to the south of the Heath, and is built around the main street which crosses the railway line and three further intersecting roads – Royal Parade, Montpelier Vale and the appealingly named Tranquil Vale. The Cator Estate – otherwise known as Blackheath Park – sits just to the south-east, while the Heath rears steeply up to the north. Somewhat surprisingly when you consider what goes on elsewhere in London, its buildings are well preserved and often of the highest quality. Quite apart from the Paragon, there are Georgian, Regency, Victorian, Edwardian and between-the-wars buildings which are as handsome as anything in this part of England. What's more, there's a sense of being in town but at the same time out in the countryside – an uncanny sensation for somewhere surrounded by Lewisham, Catford and Eltham. If the shops are a little self-admiring (small foodstores, the odd bookshop, a discreet jeweller's, several prosperous-looking estate agents and what have you) then you feel that they're probably entitled to be. The whole effect is

extremely pleasant and salubrious. And even though Blackheath
has nothing like the roll call of kings, queens, geniuses and
heroes that Greenwich can muster, it has attracted some famous
names in its relatively short life: John Stuart Mill, Charles
Gounod, Sir Arthur Eddington, the astronomer, and Nathaniel
Hawthorne himself, who lived in Pond Road in 1856.

As if to rub home its success at making the most of itself,
Blackheath has even managed to cope with the arrival of social
housing and modern architecture without losing its charm. The
Pond Road council flats (right next to salubrious Blackheath
Park) are sober, clean, orderly and handsome; while the post-war
Span developments in the centre of the Cator Estate are as fine
an expression of an age as the Paragon was of its time.

Not that they were seen as such when they were first proposed
in the 1950s. The prime mover behind the Span project was an
architect called Eric Lyons, who had become well known for his
modern house designs around Richmond and Twickenham. In
1956 he proposed building a group of new, affordable buildings on
the Cator Estate – which by this time had established itself as one
of the most quietly, traditionally affluent corners of south-east
London, with its space, its trees, its gardens and its big, handsome
villas dating from every period since the 1820s. Span's buildings,
on the other hand, were relatively modest, designed as flats, and
featured all the hallmarks of modern post-war architecture –
clean, rectilinear forms, plate-glass windows, weatherboarded
walls, colour and light. Inevitably, a huge battle began between

Lyons's supporters (who wanted, among other things, to knock down an old local landmark known as the Priory) and the traditionalists, who saw Span and everything it stood for as a premeditated affront to their way of life. The fight dragged on in a very English, middle-class fashion and in the end, as any Blackheath visitor will see, Span got its way – and the resulting buildings are wonderful, confident pieces of architecture. Indeed, by adding a fresh note to the heterogeneous mix of Blackheath Park, they lift it beyond the conventionally agreeable and make it even more interesting. Not that Lyons felt particularly well disposed to the Cator Estate by the end. In one of his buildings, he's incorporated a sculpture of a human form being crushed by the weight of the brickwork above it: symbolising, apparently, the position of the architect in society.

So the overall effect in and around Blackheath Village is a little like that of Richmond or Hampstead. But whereas Hampstead is permanently at the mercy of the traffic which churns through it (to say nothing of the thousands of visitors to Hampstead Heath and Keats's House); while Richmond has traffic and tourists (and also a constant crowd of shoppers), Blackheath keeps itself very much to itself. Quiet and affluent, it epitomises a certain kind of village-within-the-city: a very London creation.

Greenwich has always had a much more uneven hold on wealth. Walking around the centre of town, it strikes you that parts of it are almost as splendid as some of Bath, or Oxford; while right next door are parts that could come from anywhere in London, and which veer from the drably ordinary to the positively run-down.

Not that it's without its grand private buildings, to complement the grand public ones. Plainly, there was – and is – wealth in Greenwich: the merchants and entrepreneurs of the seventeenth and eighteenth centuries had money to spend and status to maintain; and they built industriously in order to make their mark. Consider, for instance, the Presbytery, on Croom's Hill. This totally unexpected redbrick Dutch-style house was put up in the 1630s by one William Smith, Sergeant-at-Arms to the king and founder of the Ship Tavern; and, with its inventive brickwork, its gables, panels and pilasters, was absolutely at the head of the seventeenth-century fashion for 'Dutch' houses. Many well-heeled and influential visitors came to admire it; although John Evelyn, on *his* visit, perversely described the house as 'a wretched one'. Hardly a rational assessment, given the building's size, elevation, prominence and stylistic boldness. Perhaps the result of pique rather than critique.

Or there's Macartney House in Chesterfield Walk, by the southern corner of the park, which sits on the sites of two earlier houses originally dating back to the second half of the seventeenth century and built, not just speculatively, but illegally, by one Andrew Snape, who simply parcelled off a piece of the king's land for himself and put up a group of private dwellings. By 1717 the older houses had been turned into one, bigger building (General Wolfe spent part of his childhood here and also lay here in state, embalmed, Nelson-like, in 1759), and in 1802 the great architect and collector, John Soane, was taken on to build a whole new front wing, with distinctive round-headed windows. It got even bigger in the mid-nineteenth century, when another extension was added to the north – and, despite various architectural manglings in the twentieth century, is still an imposing edifice.

Or, there's the Ranger's House, just along the way. Originally built for Admiral Francis Hosier, this found its way into the hands of the Fourth Earl of Chesterfield – wit, man of letters, courtier, and the person to whom Johnson wrote the famous lines, 'Is not a Patron, my Lord, one who looks with unconcern on a man struggling for life in the water, and, when he has reached ground, encumbers him with help?'; and of whose *Letters* Johnson observed, 'They teach the morals of a whore, and the manners of a dancing master'. (Chesterfield, it is well to recall at this point, once write that 'Knowledge may give weight, but accomplishments give lustre, and many more people see than weigh'.) He acquired the house – dating from 1700 – in the mid-eighteenth century and had it copiously extended, with a bay window overlooking the garden and two bow windows overlooking the Park and Blackheath – between which it sits almost at a mid-point of the whole green mass. It is brilliantly imposing and yet elegant, in the way that only English Georgian architecture can be, with its reticent brickwork given shape and drama by the stone detailing and by the assembly of classical forms and motifs around the front entrance. Even the railings and the gateway – which were added in the nineteenth century, long after Chesterfield's death – have the right mixture of restraint and delicate flamboyance. Put this together with the building's position at the crown of the world (or, at least, the crown of the world in this part of south-east London, the plateau which runs from Blackheath to the top of Shooters Hill), and you have a recipe for grandeur which even today, with the lorry fumes and the odd passing aeroplane, is hard to beat. Chesterfield himself clearly thought so. After a period of indifference, he fell in love with the spot, calling it 'My hermitage. This, I find, is my proper place'. He became a passionate gardener (he wrote about his '*furor hortensis*') and asked his friend, the diplomat Solomon Dayrolles, to send him cantaloupe melon seeds: 'It is for Blackheath that I want it.' He managed, it seems, to grow them successfully.

(Why the *Ranger's House*, incidentally? Because the official residence of the Ranger of Greenwich Park had been the Queen's House, until that building was given over to the Royal Naval Asylum in the early nineteenth century. The Ranger needed a new official residence, and Chesterfield's old home – latterly occupied by the Duchess of Brunswick – was given over for this function in 1815. Today it is an extremely agreeable museum, full of musical instruments.)

If the Ranger's House represents a certain peak of aspiration and attainment, the rest of Croom's Hill, which leads down from that high point, does its best to keep up the standard. The Presbytery may be something of an oddity among the good taste, but the rest of the hill – the first road in Greenwich to be developed for housing – is a textbook of quietly wealthy individuality. It's invidious to single out particular houses for praise or comment, since the effect of Croom's Hill is cumulative, depending on the constant flow from one building to another, the variations within the whole, and the impressive quality of the architecture on display, from the seventeenth to the nineteenth centuries. Yes, there are buildings which make you stop and stare, such as the Presbytery; or Mays Court – a wonderful late eighteenth-century terrace set back from the road behind its own green; or the Manor House. But even with these high points, it works as a whole, rewarding you, as you trudge up the slope, with glimpses and vistas, the park providing its own discourse on one side, the houses providing theirs on the other, the experience unlike just about any other in London. Perhaps Church Row in Hampstead, or some of the streets between the King's Road, Chelsea, and the Chelsea Royal Hospital might give it a run for its money. But however nice these are (and they are) they're vitiated by their surroundings, or they end too soon, or they're too full of their own importance. Nowhere has quite the richness of Croom's Hill – a street which is not just a statement of wealth and taste, but a living architectural history lesson.

And if you could somehow transfer straight from Croom's Hill to Joseph Kay's town centre, you'd have something quite unbeatable. In reality, though, it's almost impossible to look at what was known as 'The Improvement Scheme' – the block created around College Approach, King William Walk, Nelson Road and Greenwich Church Street – without having your mind distracted from the unforced appeal of the buildings by the unbelievable stream of traffic which embraces them. You name it, it grinds its way round the one-way system – buses, heavy trucks, motorbikes, wrecked old cars, tourist coaches – struggling to get on to the Romney Road or Creek Road. And Kay's quietly delicate, fastidious late Regency-style buildings just have to stand there and put up with it all.

The Improvement Scheme was the by-product of the Naval Hospital's desire to acquire some of the land on its western side and redevelop it. This area was, even in the early nineteenth century, essentially a medieval confusion of buildings, and it took a bill in Parliament to cut through the various issues of ownership and private interest and drive the process forward. Once the decision had been taken, Joseph Kay, who was already working as architect for the then new Royal Hospital School, was given the job of redesigning the town centre by means of a grand plan. The scheme got going in 1829, with the first section being completed in Nelson Road. Greenwich Market was rebuilt in 1831 and given its monumental archway entrance in College Approach at the same time. And then, with the completion of the College Approach section, there was a pause, before King William Walk and Greenwich Church Street were put up in 1843 – different from the earlier scheme in execution, but still with very much the same guiding sensibility. As a result, the centre of Greenwich has a good bit of John Nash in it, but on a smaller, more domestic scale – a scale in comparison with which Hawksmoor's St Alfege's Church, perched on the corner of the Improvement, looks even more grandiose. If you catch Kay's scheme at a moment when the traffic pauses (or early in the morning), it is immensely stylish. And if you *could* somehow arrange for it to run seamlessly into Croom's Hill and Chesterfield Walk (and, possibly, put some high-tone shops in place – jewellers, delis and dress shops, as in Blackheath), then you would have a model of the prosperous well-bred metropolitan environment. You would have a kind of urban perfection.

But of course, you can't, and it isn't. Whatever else it is, Greenwich isn't precious in that way. In fact, the mixture of rough and smooth with a maritime dressing makes it more like a south coast seaside resort. With the masts of the *Cutty Sark* towering over the riverfront buildings, the whiff of tidal water that comes up from time to time from the river, the puzzling mixture of impressive historical buildings and neglected minor ones, the cheap cafés and souvenir shops, the tour coaches and the knots of tourists consulting street plans and guidebooks, the ordinary citizens walking around with supermarket carrier bags or waiting at bus stops, it feels at times more like Brighton or Sidmouth, than anywhere in London. And that is why it can never quite catch the air of affluence which lingers around Blackheath. It's too busy with the passing trade, too much of a jumble, too bothered (like most British seaside resorts) with finding a way to do its old job in the new century. Blackheath has somehow managed to put a cordon sanitaire around itself, and exists as an island of bourgeois values. Greenwich lives more in the real world – the world of having to make ends meet, the real world defined by Deptford and Woolwich and Lewisham – and as such has to make compromises. Now, whether this is a good or a bad thing is open to question. If you could descend on Greenwich, clear away everything shabby and run-down, pedestrianise the Improvement Scheme, fill the retail outlets with the sorts of things you might find in Chelsea or Hampstead, hide the more unfortunate modern developments (the west side of Stockwell Street; Cutty Sark Gardens), and take every period building you could find (there are hundreds of them) and restore them with no expense spared – then you'd have something amounting to a single work of art, a place of unbelievable quality. But it would also be a place of unbelievable pretension. Without the roughness, without the evident human life struggling to continue, it would be like a private theme park – sterile and conceited. You have to have some sort of reality intruding, otherwise it really gets too stultifying: the problem is that Greenwich's cranky, awkward mix of heritage and real world still lacks Blackheath's suavity.

*

You can see exactly how finely balanced the problem is if you compare the Paragon in Blackheath with Gloucester Circus in Greenwich. Both were designed by the architect Michael Searles, both were built at around the same time and in the same part of London. But the way each has turned out says a lot about the two locations in which they were built.

The Paragon is Blackheath's most celebrated building. The fruit of a collaboration between John Cator (the Beckenham speculator) and Searles himself – the architect whose profession was technically no more than that of a surveyor – it was built on a site on which originally stood Sir Gregory Page's Georgian mansion, Wricklemarsh House. This cost Page £90,000 to put up in the first half of the eighteenth century and was reputedly one of the finest houses in the country; but it was sold by his heir to John Cator for a mere £22,500, and Cator, after puzzling over what to do with the property, finally pulled it down in 1787, replacing it with Searles's design.

From these somewhat awkward beginnings emerged a crescent made up of seven identical four-storey units linked by colonnades, the ends of the crescent finished by two small lodges. Even the most casual glimpse of it impresses: with its restraint, its formal self-denial (no grandiose central section; no flashy ornamentation), serving to bring out the simple drama of the curve, its proportions, it is a wonderful architectural composition. The delicate mouldings of the colonnade, and its gorgeous little Tuscan-style columns, set off and are pointed up by the bluff faces of the buildings between, surmounted by cityish mansard roofs. It is completely harmonious, entirely good taste in bricks and stone, and it still has that tension between towny urbanity and rural greenery which Searles envisaged for the project over two hundred years ago.

The whole idea was to sell Blackheath and the Paragon to city-dwellers who were tired of the noise and dirt of central London and who wanted a civilised retreat in the countryside – yet to remain within striking distance of London by boat. Which is very much the philosophy that draws people to modern Blackheath, with the substitution of railway for river transport. Moreover, it was to a certain type of city-dweller that Searles and Cator were appealing: the genteel middle-class leaseholder. Just to rub the point in, the first leases – granted at the beginning of the nineteenth century – contained all sorts of restrictions and prohibitions, even to the extent of banning the 'Art, mystery or trade' of – among other things – schoolmastering or fishmonger-ing. And when the leasehold for number 1 The Paragon was advertised in *The Times*, it was clear who the target audience was. The advertisement made heavy play of the fact that the house was 'Replete with every convenience for use, comfort and elegance', and 'Abounding with pleasant views in every direc-tion!' Well-heeled respectability was the order of the day.

For a while this worked perfectly, and the Paragon attracted precisely the kind of occupants that Searles and Cator wanted – if, that is, you exclude the notorious swindlers of Blackheath:

Eliza Robertson and Charlotte Sharpe, who occupied number 3 The Paragon in 1800, ran up a staggering £20,000 of debt and promptly did a bunk to the north of England. Apart from them, everything went according to plan. But as generations passed, things started to go downhill, and by the start of the twentieth century the Paragon was in a bad way. The houses – supremely dignified and nicely sized, but never huge – were becoming over-crowded: extra rooms had been built in, some on top of the colonnades; whole new buildings had been bodged together in the back gardens. Dubious businesses instead of respectable private owners appeared in increasing numbers. A junior school moved into number 14 during the 1920s, while a private hotel opened up at numbers 6 and 9; and an institution going by the name of The Paragon's Schools of Equitation and Ballroom Dancing appeared at number 7 at some point in the 1940s. When a succession of bombs then fell on the little crescent, it looked like the end for Cator and Searles's dream – until an architect called Charles Bernard Brown came on to the scene and began to restore the Paragon to its former glory. Between 1947 and 1957 he tidied away the excrescences of the previous century, restored the buildings which had been blown up and gave the crescent back its dignity. A plaque at one end records the fact that the restoration was given an award for merit as part of the 1951 Festival of Britain. Quite rightly. Today, the Paragon is refined, chaste, delightfully of its time (somehow it has managed to hold on to the old, frail gaslit street lamps just outside, for extra period charm), and, though divided up into flats, externally true to itself. Even the flavour of rural isolation which characterised the development two hundred years ago (the Paragon was built to be splendidly sequestered, overlooking agricultural land on the edge of the Heath) is still there, in the grassland and trees which make up the picture framed by the building's arms. It is one of Blackheath's principal attractions; and it's impossible not to see why.

But then there was Gloucester Circus, in Greenwich. Another Searles design: rather a different outcome.

At the end of the eighteenth century, the Greenwich Academy, whose headmaster was a certain Reverend A. James, stood on the three-acre site where the Circus now stands, running off Croom's Hill and leading on to Royal Hill. When the Revd James retired in 1788, he decided to form a consortium to exploit the land his school was standing on, and nominated himself as the ground landlord, with Searles as the architect and builder. This was some time before Searles began work on the nearby Paragon, and, full of enthusiasm for a large-scale project instead of the single houses he tended to design, he threw himself into the task of designing a proper Circus – very much à la mode, with two crescents facing one another across a formal garden. Unfortunately, the finances were not as straightforward as in the Cator development, and work on the first group of twenty-two houses – the south side of the circus – took forever to complete. The last of these wasn't finished until 1809, by which time Searles was nearly sixty years old and the Paragon, which started construction years later, was fully occupied. And there was still the north side of the Circus to go.

Things got worse. Not only was Searles in financial difficulties over the scheme, having sunk some of his own money into it, but the Reverend James had died. His son, a captain in the West Kent Militia, saw no future in continuing with the project – not least because the whole idea of a circus was starting to look a little unfashionable by now, a little old hat; and besides, there was more money to be made out of parcelling up the remaining land and selling it off. Which he duly did, in 1821. Other developers moved in, and a straight terrace was put up on the north side, giving the Circus its present curious D shape. Searles resigned himself to never seeing his design worked out; although he might have been cheered by the fact – had he known it – that a Second World War bomb flattened most of the north row, leaving only his south side crescent standing.

Whether he would have approved of the post-war flats that filled in the gap is another matter. These days, there's a small argument going on between Searles's original designs – with their typical neatness, modesty, fine detailing and sober proportions – and the other inhabitants of this Circus which isn't a circus. Searles's side is lovely (and the north side would look OK, anywhere else) but there's an atmosphere of regret hanging over the place that – frankly – the Paragon may have known in the late

1940s, but which it has long since overcome. Gloucester Circus could have been a little piece of Bath in south-east London, but it isn't. It could have been as exclusively high-tone as the Paragon managed to be at the outset; but it fell short.

And does this say something about the characters of Greenwich and Blackheath? Do the relative success and failure of Searles's two schemes indicate symbolically that, for the last century or so, well-heeled Blackheath has had things pretty much its own way; while Greenwich has struggled to make its extraordinary past come to terms with a rather more everyday present? Or is it that, given the sheer weight of history in Greenwich, everything has to compromise, one way or another? So much has happened there that perfection, or near-perfection, has become an impossibility. And even if you could stop time and dedicate yourself to the gradual beautification of Greenwich and the elimination of its flaws, what would you have? Something interesting, or something stultified? Is it a case of the rough edges of change versus the deadening hand of pleasant flawlessness? Is wealth, at heart, a little bit boring?

ARTY

W HAT DO we make of Greenwich Theatre? This is an instance of two worlds combining, of working-class Greenwich and refined Greenwich, the well-to-do and the humble, occupying the same spot. At least, the same spot at different times.

Greenwich Theatre sits at the foot of Croom's Hill, behind an undemonstrative foyer, next to the Rose and Crown pub. So undemonstrative is this, with its narrow portals and its uninflected late-sixties style, that it's easy to walk past without realising you've done so. But *aficionados* of theatre in Greenwich will quickly point out that this is one of the essential cultural centres of the town – both high *and* low culture – and that it has a longish and somewhat glorious past.

Back in the 1700s it was actually two separate houses, with the

Rose and Crown sandwiched in between. But by 1855 the two buildings had been converted into a skittle alley, which by 1870 was drawing big enough crowds for the landlord of the pub next door to reckon it worth converting into the Rose and Crown Music Hall. This name lasted for only a few years. The landlord, Charles Spencer Crowder, persistently searched for the most appealing combination of artistic endeavour, showbiz and self-promotion. Thus, it began as Crowder's Music Hall, boasting many interior refurbishments – including a new lavatory – and offering burlesques, ballet, and stars of the stage such as Price Barnes the Elastic Comic, and Harry Diamond, the Gem of the Coal Mines. Shortly after that, Crowder decided that he needed to branch out and expand the theatre's scope so he renamed it Crowder's Music Hall and Picture Gallery, before finally opting, in 1878, for Crowder's Music Hall and Temple of Varieties.

None of these stuck, however, and when a new landlord took over – one Alfred Ambrose Hurley – the Music Hall tag went, and it became the Parthenon Theatre of Varieties. Hurley was evidently keen to raise the tone of the place, and had it extensively rebuilt in 1885 – a symptom of changing priorities, of the genteel character of Greenwich asserting itself over the rough and ready: from skittle alley (one of the lowest forms of diversion, a long way from ten-pin bowling) to Parthenon Theatre in thirty years. Hurley plugged on with this, making improvements and additions as he went; even though on the night of the grand relaunch following one particular lot of architectural ameliorations, he was chagrined to find that, despite having drawn a sell-out crowd, the London County Council wouldn't let him open until he had the ceiling plastered. Still, he struggled on until the theatre changed hands again in 1900, becoming the Greenwich Palace of Varieties, and hosting a galaxy of stars, to say nothing of an Edison phonograph. But this lasted only a few years, before the theatre changed hands *again*. Two new proprietors took over in 1903 – Samuel and Daniel Barnard, who felt that the classical overtones were putting off more people than they were pulling in: so they reorientated the place once more, encouraging the paying public in with pantomimes and popular musicals. Did this incarnation stick? Naturally not. The place was so resistant to keeping one name that by 1915 the Greenwich Palace of Varieties had become the Greenwich Hippodrome Picture Palace and found itself, more often than not, showing movies rather than live dramatic spectacles. After the end of the Second World War it lost its music hall licence and became a cinema pure and simple – but even then was too small and too awkward for the big screen effects coming in. So it closed down in 1949 – its empty auditorium being used for warehousing. It was, in fact, dying: a one-hundred-year career had ground to a halt, and the whole building, with its charming high Victorian décor by John Buckle, was falling apart.

But then it found a saviour. An actor called Ewan Hooper (you can see him in the 1968 horror flick *Dracula Has Risen from the Grave*, with Christopher Lee as the vampire) devoted most of the 1960s to bringing it back to life. This was a quintessential sixties thing to do: the affluence of the time coincided with a desire to restore and preserve the heritage of the past in the face of apparently random rebuilding and reconstruction. The splendid old Greenwich Hippodrome would have been a prime target for the ambitions of the community, no matter how uneven or inconsistent its history had been. And it was a heroic undertaking. Seven years of persistence and unstoppable fund-raising saw the building reopen in 1969 as the Greenwich Theatre, with a musical, *Martin Luther King*, followed by a documentary play about the Spithead Mutiny, an Iris Murdoch drama, and – a real feather in its cap – the stage première of John Mortimer's *A Voyage Round My Father*. It boasted a hexagonal thrust stage, seating for over 400 people, a restaurant, an art gallery (a whiff of Charles Spencer Crowder, there) and a separate touring company working under its aegis. It was a tremendous achievement, and without a doubt, one in the eye for Blackheath, with its grand Arts and Crafts style 1895 Concert Hall – which had to wait until 1985 for *its* formal reopening.

However an enterprise on this scale needs central funding to exist in the modern world. And despite the relative prominence of the Greenwich Theatre – especially in south-east London, where it is the only professional producing house in the region – after some thirty years of highly successful business it had its annual grant withdrawn. Fourteen national tours, annual audiences averaging 68,000, a surplus on its accounts – all failed to save it, and it went dark in March 1998. At the time of writing, a campaign is under way to get it going again and generate the sense of cultural purpose and identity that somewhere like Greenwich depends on – much as Wimbledon and Richmond rely on their theatres to confirm their respectives senses of place. Running a theatre – anywhere in London – is an expensive and precarious business; and it can only be an adornment to a community to have a living theatre at its heart.

The Greenwich Theatre story also suggests something else about Greenwich as a whole. It points up the odd relationship it has always had with writers, artists – and the arts in general. The place seems to fascinate, but in a haphazard fashion. For centuries, writers have found themselves living and working in Greenwich, for any number of odd reasons. Samuel Pepys, for instance, was constantly in and around the place as a result of his position in the Navy, which led him from Whitehall up and down the Thames on a regular basis. Greenwich crops up in his *Diaries* even more persistently once the Plague sets in, in 1665, and he moves his wife out of central London to the fresher airs of Kent: 'Advised about sending my wife's bedding and things today,' he writes, on 5 July, 'to Woolwich, in order to her removal thither.' From then on, Greenwich and its neighbours litter his entries. 'Come letters from the King and Lord Arlington,' he writes, on 19 August 1665, 'for the removal of our office to Greenwich.' On the 20th he dolefully recounts: 'Walked to Greenwich, in my way seeing a coffin with a dead body therein, dead of the plague, lying in an open close belonging to Coome farme, which was carried out last night, and the parish have not appointed any body to bury it; but only set a watch there all day and night, that nobody should go thither or come thence: this disease making us more cruel to one another than we are to dogs.' This is qualified by his entry for the 21st, in which he goes 'To my Lord Brouncker, at Greenwich, to look after the lodgings appointed for us there for our office, which do by no means please us; they being in the heart of all the labourers and work-men there, which makes it as unsafe as to be, I think, at London . . .' On 28 November he 'Took boat, and down to Greenwich. Cocke home, and I to the office, and then to my lodgings, where my wife is come, and I am well pleased with it, only much trouble in those lodgings we have, the mistress of the house being so deadly dear in everything we have.' Yet again, on 31 December: 'It is true we have gone through great melancholy because of the great plague, and I put to great charges by it, by keeping my family long at Woolwich; and myself and another part of my family, my clerks, at my charge, at Greenwich, and a maid at London; but I hope the King will give us some satisfac-tion for that.' He returns to London, but is driven out again by the Great Fire of 1666, this time making sure of his most impor-tant possession – money – first: 'Took my gold, which was about

£2,350, W. Hewer and Jane down by Proudy's boat to Woolwich; but Lord! what a sad sight it was by moone-light, to see the whole City almost on fire, that you might see it as plain at Woolwich, as if you were by it . . .'

Yet Pepys's relationship with Greenwich is somehow tangential and anomalous. He was accidentally drawn to Greenwich; and it was entirely fortuitous that his diaries should have been transcribed, edited and published in the nineteenth century and that we should know of his connection with the place. He saw himself as an industrious Crown administrator, rather than a writer – yet it's his fame as a diarist that adds lustre to the reputation of Greenwich: an oddity, really.

Dickens and Wilkie Collins, writers above all else, were both *habitués* of Greenwich riverside life. Likewise Captain Frederick Marryat, best known for his novel *Mr Midshipman Easy*, whose *Poor Jack* was partly set in Greenwich. George Cruikshank, the illustrator responsible for the drawings in Dickens's *Sketches by Boz* and *Oliver Twist*, was a fan of the place, too; as was the poet, essayist and historian, Lord Macaulay. They were all, if you like, much more Greenwich writers than Pepys. Drawn there by what? Its riverside loucheness, perhaps; its mixture of green and grime, London but not London – qualities which can't easily be replicated anywhere else along the Thames. Dickens, as we've seen, would have responded particularly to the democratic, free-for-all atmosphere, its potential for cheerfully vulgar holiday pleasure-seeking.

C. Day-Lewis, on the other hand, could hardly have been more refined. He was the author of, among other things, these lines:

> The slow movement of clouds in benediction,
> Clear arias of light thrilling over her uplands,
> Over the chords of summer sustained peacefully

Day-Lewis epitomises a certain kind of English culture – the antithesis of what Dickens came to represent. In a more or less wholly illustrious life, Day-Lewis was Oxford Professor of Poetry, and subsequently held the same chair at Harvard, before being appointed Poet Laureate in 1968. He translated Virgil, generated a number of important critical works and was like *that* with W. H. Auden and Stephen Spender. The aesthetic, literary intelligence in human form, in many ways – and until his death in 1972 he lived at number 6 Croom's Hill, just opposite the Greenwich Theatre and a stone's throw from the *Cutty Sark*.

Now, this kind of existence is a long way from Dickensian rough-and-ready living down by the river. It is a highly refined life, lived in one of the most handsome houses on the hill (built in 1718), a really exquisite piece of Georgian town building (so exquisite, in fact, that the award-winning Fan Museum took over the two houses at the end of Day-Lewis's terrace in the early 1990s to house its collection, displaying it in immaculately restored surroundings, an unlikely but entirely passionate celebration of a specific art, the only one of its kind in the world). This is a Greenwich a long way removed from day trippers and pleasure-seekers and conspicuous consumption in the Trafalgar Tavern. This is arty Greenwich: there must have been something in the atmosphere to keep Day-Lewis there, when he could easily have gone to Hampstead or Chelsea – somewhere more obviously a metropolitan cultural hotbed. This also suggests itself in the unusual number of second-hand bookshops dotted around Greenwich and Blackheath (especially when you consider how thinly supplied the area is with more mainstream shops), and in the historical and cultural societies that keep going. Many recent writers and artists (Day-Lewis aside) have lived in and around the place, John Bratby and Michael Frayn being two of the more prominent. The outer fringes of Greenwich are colonised by journalists, jazz buffs, collectors, bohos who settle in large Victorian villas in streets like Granville Park or Oakcroft Road, on the Blackheath/Lewisham border. And Greenwich appeals to film-makers, over and over again. Not just for period settings – as in *The Madness of King George* and *Sense and Sensibility* – but for modern-dress dramas such as *Sunday Bloody Sunday* (set in Blackheath), *Four Weddings and a Funeral* (admittedly, modern dress in the Royal Naval College Chapel) and, strangest of all, *Blow-Up*.

Blow-Up, made in 1966 by Michelangelo Antonioni, is a glossy, infuriating masterpiece, set in the purest, mid-sixties swinging London. It centres around a David Bailey-esque fashion photographer (played by David Hemmings), who finds that he may or may not have accidentally photographed a murder which may or may not have taken place. Much of the film is set in the photographer's chic studio, or in fashionable restaurants, or at happening, drug-filled parties. But the actual murder – if such it is – is committed in Maryon Park, just north of the immortal Charlton House. Not that the place is ever identified, but Antonioni – who was obsessed with portraying the surface of reality in a very specific way, and who wanted to play around with the whole idea of appearances and actualities – decided that Maryon Park was the perfect exterior setting in which the Hemmings character could take mood photographs – in the corners of which lurk the evidence for the crime which may (or may not) have happened.

Maryon Park – named after the Maryon-Wilson family, the last private owners of Charlton House – was created by the London County Council at the end of the nineteenth century, as a much-needed piece of open land in what was then a mass of poor housing, industrial grime and generally unhealthy living conditions. The LCC took 12 acres of disused chalk, sand and gravel pits, grassed them over, and presented the park to the people. In 1895 a children's playground was added: boasting all the modern attractions of swings and climbing-frames, it was advertised as an 'Open-air gymnasium'. Tennis courts were laid, trees planted, and by the 1960s Maryon Park was green, leafy and a pleasant break in the continuing urbanisation of south-east

London. So why did Antonioni pick it as the arena for the central act of his film?

Because there's definitely something strange about it. Quite apart from the fact that it was the site of a Romano-British settlement with banks, ditches and hut dwellings, its later career as a quarry has left it full of short, steep slopes, mysterious mounds and platforms of grass looking down on the surrounding land. And it was one of these half-natural, half-artificial grass stages that the director used as a setting for the murder, and where David Hemmings snapped on a strange, whispering summer's day. The effect is heightened in the film by a row of fake buildings Antonioni put up to close off the skyline; by the green paint he lavished on the park railings, for extra tranquil verdancy; and by the stylised soundtrack – no noise, no traffic sounds, no passing aeroplanes or people's voices, just the constant whispering and rustling of the trees. The result is hypnotic, completely disorientating. The light, too, is slightly odd for London. It's both illuminating and concealing, a very strange combination. You can see perfectly, everything is in focus: except that you can't see what you *want* to see. There's a secrecy about the area. It's as if Antonioni, the outsider, picked up a third kind of Greenwich – not the pleasurable, entertaining, riverside Greenwich of Dickens, or the refined, aesthetic Greenwich where Day-Lewis lived; but a place whose obscurity and sense of being slightly off the map he could turn to his own ends. There *is* an enigmatic quality to this part of the world (the timeless presence of the river helps) and he tapped into it, exaggerated it and made it a central component in a mystery film which is so enigmatic itself that it is at times impenetrable.

In this part of London you're off the beaten track (only now has it been connected to the London Underground system, for instance), on the way to nowhere special – and yet it has enough history, architecture, heritage, sense of place and natural environmental resources (from the river to the scatterings of heaths and parks) to make it a place worth living in. You're in London, but not necessarily *of* London; you're not trapped by it. It's a place for artistic individualists.

Two of whom have left monuments to themselves at opposite ends of town.

The area now known as Westcombe is a patch of sheer, unremarkable outer London, a vague square bounded by the Woolwich Road, the motorway which leads into the Blackwall Tunnel, Shooters Hill and the Maze Hill edge of Greenwich Park. There's no immediate, clear reason to go there. Except that at the southern end of Mycenae Road stands one of those glum Victorian-looking villas you see all over the outskirts of London, too big for any private individual, too awkward to be made into user-friendly modern apartments. This one belonged to John Julius Angerstein, a man who made a deep impact not only on Greenwich but on the whole of London, culturally and economically.

In the second half of the eighteenth century, Angerstein (reputedly the illegitimate son of Empress Anne of Russia), having arrived from his birthplace of St Petersburg in 1750, found employment at Thomas's Counting House in the City. This led him into a vital association with London's nascent insurance market, in the shape of the still-juvenile Lloyd's of London. This was badly organised, incapable of dealing adequately with the business that was starting to come its way, and without a permanent home. Angerstein – not even a member of Lloyd's at this stage, but a mere subscriber – cut through the ineffectuality and dithering that had paralysed the Lloyd's Committee, found the institution permanent premises in the Royal Exchange and (for good or bad) institutionalised the Lloyd's practice of doing business through individual underwriters. For this, he became known as 'The Father of Lloyd's'.

In 1774 he had a substantial house designed for him by George Gibson and erected at the top of Maze Hill so that he could gaze down, in the approved fashion, on the river. Known as Woodlands, this was Angerstein's Greenwich seat, a 'charming little villa' visited by George III and rapidly filled up by Angerstein's family, when they weren't occupying his London residence at 100 Pall Mall. It was here and in London that Angerstein, assisted by artists such as Joshua Reynolds and Benjamin West (the painter of the St Paul altarpiece in the Royal Naval College Chapel) started to establish a private collection of Old Master paintings. By the end of his life he had acquired a core of thirty-eight important works of art by, among others, Claude, Rubens, Rembrandt, Van Dyck and Raphael. Displayed at Woodlands and in Pall Mall, this collection was a major piece of art connoisseurship – so much so, that on his death Angerstein directed that it should be sold intact, unless it remained in this country; in which case it should be bought by the government for the nation. After the usual delaying and head-scratching, the government finally acceded, paid £60,000 for the collection, took over the lease of the house at 100 Pall Mall, and in 1824 hung the paintings on public display. This was Britain's first National Gallery: the thirty-eight paintings collected by John Julius Angerstein.

(Woodlands, meanwhile, was altered and enlarged by subsequent owners, becoming a convent for the Little Sisters of the Assumption between 1923 and 1967. The London Borough of Greenwich then took it over, turning it into an art gallery and local history library. The Angerstein name, meanwhile, became attached to the extensive riverside development on the eastern shores of the Greenwich Peninsula – Angerstein Wharf – which grew so large in the nineteenth century that it had to build its own Angerstein branch line to run goods trains into the main railway line to the south – a branch line which was still going, late into the twentieth century.)

But if Angerstein was something of an aesthete, what does that make Sir John Vanbrugh? Born in 1664, Vanbrugh was an astonishingly creative personality. Having spent a few formative years as a soldier, he turned his hand to writing comedy – and scored two immediate, scandalising hits: *The Relapse* ('Egad, old dad, I'll put my hand in thy bosom now!'), followed by *The Provok'd Wife* ('Ay, but you know we must return good for evil' – 'That may be a mistake in the translation'). The stage, however, could not hold him for ever, and after a brief pause his career changed direction. He became an architect, and got off to a surprising start when, working in tandem with Nicholas Hawksmoor, he designed Castle Howard on the edge of the North York Moors. This building, one of the pinnacles of English baroque, is a dazzling combination of Vanbrugh's sense of heroic scale and plan, with Hawksmoor's realisation of the individual effects which combine to create the whole. On the strength of this triumph, Vanbrugh was appointed Comptroller of the Queen's Works, and in 1705 was picked by the First Duke of Marlborough to design one of the greatest private homes in the world – Blenheim Palace, in Oxfordshire.

Which Vanbrugh duly did – along, once again, with Hawksmoor – creating a masterpiece in the process. Unfortunately, the Duchess of Marlborough didn't see it the same way, and the association ended in acrimony. But Vanbrugh had established an imperishable reputation. He was knighted in 1714, and when he was appointed Surveyor to the Royal Naval Hospital after Wren in 1716 he was accepting a position to which most people thought him perfectly suited. By this stage, the hospital was well on the way to completion, and Vanbrugh's contribution – apart from overseeing the building works – is mainly found in the last section to be finished: the quirky elevations, a reworking of the motifs of classicism, at the rear of the hospital along the Romney Road. Having found himself in Greenwich at the age of fifty-five, and with a longish task ahead of him, he decided to construct himself a suitable home – not too far from work, and with a pleasant view. The result was Vanbrugh Castle, halfway up Maze Hill, a short walk from the later Woodlands and overlooking Greenwich Park.

Now, there is no shortage of competition for the title of Oddest Building in Greenwich, but Vanbrugh Castle must surely be one of the front-runners. Built in 1719, it is inexplicably peculiar, and totally unlike anything else around it. Which may well have been the idea: Vanbrugh's sense of drama – massively realised at Castle Howard and Blenheim – had to shrink to fit a much smaller spot in east Greenwich. But at east he could make the neighbours stare at the exact opposite of the baroque classicism of the Royal Naval Hospital, the cool Palladianism of the Queen's House and the Georgian prettiness of the expanding Croom's Hill. Instead, he put up a miniature Scottish castle, complete with castellated towers, daunting brickwork, a central tower with a lead cone on the top, and whimsically narrowed windows, somewhere between conventional eighteenth-century practice and Gothic arrow slits. Even though various additions have been tacked on over the years – the south wing, and a startlingly inappropriate white classical porch at the front door –

it's still Vanbrugh's central fortress that strikes you, stopping you short and making you wonder what eccentric was responsible for it. Vanbrugh also built an estate of baby castle-shaped villas to go with the main building – all of which have since been knocked down. It was clearly an idea he was in love with.

And it's not just a *jeu d'esprit* (even though in some eyes its main claim to fame is precisely that it is Britain's first proper architectural folly). No matter how silly it may look it is historically important, in that it revived the medieval look at a time when classical order and the virtuous restraint of the eighteenth century were universal. It was a romantic gesture right in the middle of the Age of Reason, and as such, prefigured the Gothic revivalism that swept Britain from the end of the eighteenth century and all through the nineteenth. No one would claim that it's equal in importance to Inigo Jones's Queen's House; but without a doubt, Vanbrugh was well ahead of his time, anticipating the fashion and adding one more extraordinary building to the collection massed in SE10. The epitome of Greenwich individualism, Vanbrugh made his statement; and lived in it until his death in 1726.

CONSUMER

I T WOULD PROBABLY be fair to admit that eating and drinking and shopping in Greenwich suffered somewhat as the twentieth century wore on. The famous riverside whitebait taverns closed down, the restaurants in the centre came and went, postwar redevelopments did nothing to make Greenwich the consumer capital of south-east London.

Consider, for instance, the tale of the Ship.

For centuries, the Ship was a Greenwich institution – even a national institution, so celebrated was it by lovers of food and drink. The earliest recorded Ship Tavern stood at the east end of Tavern Row, a street at one time enclosed within the grounds of the Royal Naval Hospital. As well as serving comestibles to passing travellers and local residents, it was, as was the custom, also an inn. Back in the seventeenth century, it was used as a temporary prison: sixty suspected witches – the so-called Lancashire Witches – were held there, pending their trial by a team of midwives appointed by the Royal Surgeons. As it turned out, the midwives found none of the physical signs on the women that would have proved their guilt and so King Charles I was obliged to pardon them – none of which lurid folk history helped the Ship, as it was pulled down in the eighteenth century and replaced with a new brick and timber construction in Fisher Lane. This new Ship was much favoured by Westminster politicians, who made the river journey from the centre of town specifically to eat its famed whitebait dishes, but in the fullness of time this Ship too was pulled down. Nevertheless, in a typical historical elision, the old Torbay Tavern at the end of King William Walk took over the name, becoming the third Ship and continuing the whitebait tradition. In the mid-nineteenth century, this Ship found itself involved in a fierce legal fight with the Royal Hospital, which wanted to pull the inn down in order to extend its own grounds. In the course of the action, it emerged that the Ship at Greenwich was serving the most profitable whitebait dinners in the country. In a single day, the landlady would serve some forty whitebait orders at 2s. 6d. each, netting her a gross take of £5. Total cost of the fish required? Three shillings and sixpence. Allowing for overheads, her mark-up was around 2,000 per cent.

The Naval Hospital had its way, the third Ship was pulled down, and the fourth, last and grandest Ship was built between

King William Walk and Church Street. This was a true Victorian heavyweight. It contained dining-rooms named after Nelson and Wellington, seven private rooms, a billiard room and a ballroom lit by gas chandeliers designed for the Great Exhibition. From its opening at the end of the 1850s to the turn of the century, it did the same prosperous business as before – feeding government ministers (generally speaking, Tories) their vast whitebait feasts, and, according to Charles Dickens, serving up a total of 30,000 flounders during the summer season. City livery companies, sporting clubs and learned societies all booked its private rooms and spent small fortunes there.

But by the beginning of the twentieth century it had lost its appeal, and business was declining. Lord Rosebery – Secretary for Foreign Affairs in the Gladstone administration, and subsequently leader of the Liberal Party – had signalled the beginning of the end in 1894, when he held the last ministerial celebration at the Ship. From then on, the decline was amazingly swift and by 1908 it was forced to close down completely and was reduced to auctioning off its splendid contents. Sale posters of the time refer poignantly to 'Fine old mahogany furniture', 'Two very handsome 15-light ballroom chandeliers', 'The whole of the extensive collection of Old Sheffield Plate', and 'Costly overmantels and pier glasses' – all of which were stripped from the interior and dispersed throughout the country. The auction over, the Ship closed, the rear half of the building was pulled down and thirteen houses were erected in its place. It did manage to reopen not long after, in a reduced way, but by this time was clearly an anachronism, doomed to fail. Its physical size (three daunting storeys plus a mansard), its profusion of services and its looming Victorian neo-classical ornamentation (looking in some photographs as if it's been thieved from the Naval Hospital) all belonged to another age. And when a bomb fell on it in 1941 it was, in one sense, the least bad ending: the old building was put out of its misery, leaving a convenient space in which to put the *Cutty Sark*.

But the Ship was only one of a triumvirate of waterfront whitebait taverns. Just past the Royal Naval Hospital stood the Trafalgar Tavern, and just beyond that, the Crown and Sceptre. All three were in direct competition, on exactly the same stretch of the Greenwich waterfront and offering the same mixture of fresh fish and riverside interest. The Crown and Sceptre was the first to go, being pulled down in the 1930s along with the Conservative Club next door. Judging from contemporary photographs, however good its meals may have been, it must have cut the least impressive dash of the three taverns. It has a strong whiff of the shanty town, with its copious dark weatherboarding, rickety oriel windows and a flagpole out at the front. The Yacht pub, upstream, was not that much better – certainly not in comparison with its neighbour the Trafalgar Tavern – but at least it had a marginally more permanent appearance, as well as a fine roof terrace overlooking the river. Nevertheless, Dickens's diaries and correspondence reveal him eating at the Crown and Sceptre in July 1837, at a Literary Fund dinner; and in May 1848 at a reunion of the Theatrical Company – which cost a hefty 25 shillings a head.

The Trafalgar Tavern was evidently the star of the riverfront – and, once you've taken the *Cutty Sark* and the Royal Naval College into account, still is. Designed by Joseph Kay, the man responsible for the grand Improvement Scheme, it was built in 1837 in a majestic Regency style, and was so large that it covered a site previously occupied by the whole of the old George pub and six adjoining cottages. This was a truly splendid place in which to entertain, and, like the later Ship, it gave its dining-rooms imposing and historically charged names to add to its grandeur: Nelson, Hardy, Victory, Nile and, naturally, Trafalgar. The Nelson room was tricked out to resemble the stern galley of HMS *Victory*, boasting lanterns, sloping walls, and balustrades made of carved oak. In a tank, live turtles swam haplessly about for the customers to choose from; while the silvery whitebait – the main reason for the river trip down to Greenwich – could be caught, cooked and served within the hour. Not that turtles and whitebait were the only dishes on offer. When Macaulay ate there, he is known on at least one occasion to have dispatched not just a mass of fried whitebait, but also a number of spitch-cocked eels (cut up, then fried in herbs and breadcrumbs) plus a stewed carp. It was a place of prodigal, Victorian self-indulgence.

Dickens was its most ardent admirer. Not only did he eat there on a relatively workaday basis, but he also held his celebration dinner there on his return from the United States in 1842, and used it (garnished with approval) as a setting in *Our Mutual Friend*. In this, it appears as the place where Pa and Bella Wilfer have their dinner together – 'The little room overlooking the river into which they were shown for dinner was delightful. Everything was delightful. The park was delightful, the punch was delightful, the dishes of fish were delightful, the wine was delightful' – and also at the marriage feast of Bella and John Rokesmith. 'The marriage dinner,' he writes, 'was the crowning success, for what had bride and bridegroom plotted to do, but to have and to hold that dinner in the very room of the very hotel where Pa and the lovely woman had once dined together! . . . What a dinner! Specimens of all the fishes that swim in the sea surely had swum their way to it . . . And the dishes, being seasoned with Bliss – an article which they are sometimes out of at Greenwich – were of perfect flavour . . . Never-to-be-forgotten Greenwich!'

But even the Trafalgar hit hard times, and closed down in 1915, reopening not long after as the headquarters of the Royal Alfred Seamen's Institution. In the 1920s it was taken over by the Engineers' Club, only to be catastrophically flooded in 1928 when the billiard room was engulfed by two feet of 'mud, slime and wreckage'. Soon after that it turned into a centre for the unemployed, where, for a penny a week, you could have a cheap meal, attend classes and mend the family's shoes. A picture from the time shows its drab western aspect, the stucco cracked, the paint peeling, GREENWICH CENTRE FOR UNEMPLOYED MEN on the wall, the street outside empty of life. Following *that* it became a temporary fire station; and then was turned into a makeshift apartment block. It wasn't until 1965 that sense prevailed, and the building was refurbished and brought back to life as a pub and restaurant: some way from the giddy heights of Dickens's times, but one of Greenwich's indisputable treasures, it is as charged with significance as the Neptune Hall or the Ranger's House, in 1996 even gaining the accolade of *Evening Standard* Pub of the Year.

The problem is, finding anything to equal it. Greenwich is simply not a great place to eat. There are some nice pubs, a few Chinese, Thai and Indian restaurants, Goddard's Pie House, the cafés attached to the Royal Observatory and the Maritime Museum, some chip shops. The passing visitor has plenty of places to choose from, none of them particularly remarkable. All the excitement is provided by the buildings and the location; none by the gastronomy.

Which is also, to an extent, true of the shopping opportunities. Like all British towns, Greenwich has had to battle with the changing face of retailing, its high street character waning as time has gone by. In the nineteenth century, Greenwich would have been a centre for most purchasing needs – not least because just beyond the industrialisation of the riverside there were acres and acres of farm and open land whose inhabitants still needed the resources of a proper small town. Greenwich offered the services of bankers, brokers, goldsmiths, a wine merchant, drapers, milliners, a haberdasher, a furrier, bootmaker, a pair of oilmen – quite apart from the essentials of butcher, grocer, fishmonger and poulterer. To look at pictures of Victorian and Edwardian Greenwich is to mourn the loss of a whole world; a world in which buildings were fitted for their purpose, and trade went on in an atmosphere of apparently quiet, serviceable endeavour. In addition to the elaborate shop fronts (*Professor Wallis, Hair Dresser & Perfumer*; *Chocolates & Pastries* next door; *Mr Thompson, Champion Pie Maker* with his shop in St Alphege Passage), itinerant vendors add colour to the scene. Crockery salesmen bring up their barrows, laden with plates and bowls packed in straw; the sherbet seller sets up her canteen by the park: 'Sherbet – ha'penny a glass.' Even photographs taken much later – in the 1930s and 1950s – have the same harmonious qualities. A 1937 view down Stockwell Street, for instance, shows the tower of St Alfege's rising solemnly above the rooftops, the road leading to it broad and empty of traffic, while individuals and groups of figures go about their business and shops ply their trade: the newsagent's and tobacconist's frantic with placards for Player's Weights and Will's Gold Flake; the dairy next door well covered against the light of the sun; the milkman's picturesque cart parked by the pavement . . . and so on. It is an unusual assemblage of homely buildings, shop awnings, and the wedding-cake top of the church (the least gloomy part of Hawksmoor's building – not surprisingly: the tower was designed by John

James), with the wide street linking them all, and only a couple of parked cars in sight.

Cars are, of course, the key to the lost urban idyll. After the war came attempts at rebuilding and replanning Greenwich and the surrounding area, and, as in most of Britain, nothing was done terribly well or sympathetically. Still, it could have been worse. At the end of the 1960s the council had got it into its head to push a motorway through the town centre, link up with Thamesmead, east of Woolwich, and have a nineteen-lane inter-section in front of St Alfege's, all in the name of revitalising south-east London; fortunately, the scheme ran out of money before it ever began. What they did do, as anyone will tell you, is drive a punishing one-way system through the centre of town, round the Improvement Scheme and off down the Romney Road in one direction and Creek Road in the other, with offshoots up the High Road and South Street. Depressingly, this has now become the single most dominant feature of the town. Impossible to imagine in, say, Germany or France, where it would be pedes-trianised, landscaped, kept clean and dotted with cafés – but here it is, in one of UNESCO's World Heritage sites, an endless, ungoverned stream of traffic. Tourists are funnelled out of buses and ushered across the streets, from *Cutty Sark* to Maritime Museum, up the tranquil relief of the park, then downhill again into King William Walk, the traffic and their waiting coaches. Inducements to stop and enjoy the scene, to linger around the shops and restaurants, to stroll and eat an ice-cream in the centre of Greenwich are almost nil. Just window shopping is a nerve-racking experience, given the fact that the pavements are narrow (so everyone has to fight their way past; or you have to fight your way past them) and that crossing from one side of the street to another is a matter of life and death, dodging the speeding traffic.

The shops that remain are an odd assortment, aimed mainly at tourists and the occasional serious student of culture. There is that unusual number of second-hand and specialist bookshops (some, reasonably enough, specialising in nautical and maritime texts), a sprinkling of discount bookshops, the odd nautical memorabilia shop, tourist gift shops, some general food and drink supermarts in a space near the station and, tucked away from the main strip, the occasional old-fashioned butcher and greengrocer.

Where it does come into its own is in the Market. Of all the parts of central Greenwich to have been through the ravages of the twentieth century, the Market has managed the transition best. It's part of Joseph Kay's Improvement Scheme, dating from 1831, and with its simple-but-noble archway, its comfortable proportions and its neat cobbles has an atmosphere of unthreatening, manageable mercantile enthusiasm. The fact is, nevertheless, that it's changed in character an awful lot since the days when it was a general market for the people of Greenwich town. In the past it sold fruit and veg, fish, meat, clothing; it lent money and it had a pawnbroker's. It was a market in the way that supermarkets are now markets – everything under one roof (which actually dates from 1908) and no pretensions. Better yet is the motto above the archway, which reads, A FALSE BALANCE IS AN ABOMINATION TO THE LORD, BUT A JUST WEIGHT IS HIS DELIGHT. The neat little shops around the edge of the Market date from 1958, when it became a fruit and vegetable market only, whereas the older shops and pubs on the outside, in Turnpin Lane, really do have a foot in the past; not least because Turnpin Lane claims to be the most ancient alley in Greenwich, following a medieval street line. The atmosphere of this small block is quite different to the mood of the rest of the town centre: only a few yards from the maelstrom of traffic outside, but profoundly quiet in comparison, locked in a time before cars.

Whether or not you approve of what the Market now sells is another matter. The little shops open on and off during the week, but the real business is done at weekends, when the Market proper takes place. And this is very much your London amusement market, selling absolutely nothing essential, but strong on hand-crafted jewellery, scarves, framed prints, sweetmeats, delicatessen delights, candles, antiquarian books, unique bits of pottery. It is shopping as tourism and leisure, and it spreads into the surrounding streets, pitching itself on more or less any level piece of ground and sneaking into any building with space to handle it. Naturally this free-form bric-à-bric business has experienced changes in the past decades. Back in the 1970s, one vast open-air market took over a patch of land in the Greenwich High Road each weekend, and generated so much business on so many stalls that visitors arrived by the coachload, just for the browsing. So popular was this offspring of the covered Market that it had to be curtailed. The site was redeveloped: a new cinema was built on it, and the open-air market was sidelined to a minor car park round the back. All the same, the desire of people to come and pick over junk at the weekends is so strong, and the desire of traders to get down to SE10 so overwhelming, that by one estimate, every weekend sees no fewer than eleven separate markets dotted around Greenwich, ranging from the glamorous one in Joseph Kay's old building, to a huddle of tables and stands lurking on an unused triangle of pavement some-where up Stockwell Street.

SCIENTIFIC I

DESPITE THE immense, assertive presence of the Royal Naval College; despite the genius of the Queen's House; despite the great, sullen Thames, coiling around the Isle of Dogs; it's hard to imagine anywhere in Greenwich more engrossing, more simply magical, than the Old Royal Observatory perched on the top of Greenwich Hill. The sense of occasion, of mystery, is strongest at a time when the rest of Greenwich is at its gloomiest and least prepossessing. If you visit the Old Observatory in winter, on a cold and blustery day, when the flood of tourists has reduced to a trickle and the feeling is that you are alone on the roof of London, away from the everyday world – then the atmosphere can be strange and affecting. Flamsteed's jewel-like house is empty and silent, apart from the wind whistling around corners and through gaps. The cold, bleak observation rooms – Halley's

Quadrant Room, Bradley's Transit Room, Airy's Transit Circle –
seem even colder and bleaker, reminding you of the long, lonely
chilly hours that the astronomers and their assistants spent
recording their findings. The Great Equatorial Building, with its
weird onion dome and the monstrous yet delicate refracting telescope at its centre, echoes and whispers. The beautiful Octagon
Room, a *jeu d'esprit* by Wren, yet a wonderful attempt to marry
form and function, is as still and uplifting as any church, but
with the clouds racing by the huge windows and the light restlessly changing by the minute. And throughout the whole
complex of rooms and buildings, the overwhelming significance
of it all hangs in the air: this is a place which has only ever concerned itself with universal questions of space and time, a place
which is both humbling and inspirational.

The search for a reliable method of calculating longitude was
behind it all. Back in the days when navigation at sea was guess-
work as much as science – when Drake was circumnavigating the
globe, for instance – it was nonetheless relatively easy to establish latitude: how far north or south you were on the surface of
the earth. From the early Middle Ages onwards, mariners used
astrolabes and quadrants, and from the sixteenth century cross-
staffs and sextants – all more or less reliable ways of determining
the altitude of the Pole Star, or noonday sun. From that, latitude
could be worked out with the help of an almanac.

The big problem was to determine how far round the globe

you had travelled in an easterly or westerly direction: longitude. For centuries, it had been accepted that the lunar method of calculation – measuring the angular displacement of the moon from other celestial bodies – was the one most likely to work. But the lunar method needed detailed and accurate mapping of the heavens – years of very high-quality observations, in fact, before satisfactory astronomical tables would be available. Moreover, the lunar method, even with accurate tables, was a complicated and time-consuming way of fixing the information needed out at sea.

All of which meant potential disaster, every time a ship set sail. It would leave its home port – at Penzance, say – and head south. After a few days, the captain might have an idea how far south he had gone, but only a limited idea of how far west. How quickly was it moving towards its destination – let's say, the Azores? For centuries, sea captains had relied on the method known as dead reckoning – throwing a log overboard and gaining a rough idea of the ship's speed by seeing how quickly a rope to which the log was attached paid itself out from the ship. Knots tied at regular lengths in the rope gave a rough measure – the *knots* still referred to by all mariners. An interval of twenty seconds elapsed, and then the number of knots was counted up and a semi-accurate sea speed was calculated. A compass, or a reading of the stars, plus a vague idea of time – from an hourglass, or pocket watch – came into the reckoning. And that was it. At the end of the procedure the captain could have only a very approximate notion of where he was on the featureless ocean. Was the ship a long way out from land, or not as far as the captain thought? Were they even going to overshoot their destination? And if that happened, how would they replenish their vital stocks of food and water? What if they drifted into the hands of pirates? Pirates were in fact one of the most pressing problems, along with scurvy and death by shipwreck (for example the Scilly Isles catastrophe of 1707, when Admiral Sir Cloudesley Shovel and nearly 2,000 of his seamen drowned), as ships tended to congregate in the known and most reliable trade routes, where brigands could also loiter, waiting to make a killing.

By the mid-seventeenth century the search for a reliable way of determining longitude was becoming progressively more intense, as all the major sea powers – France, Britain, the Netherlands, Spain and Italy – were anxious to give their seamen this crucial advantage in navigation. Charles II had already set up a committee to examine the problem when a French astronomer called Le Sieur de St Pierre claimed, in the early 1670s, to have established a foolproof method using vertical angles to measure the moon's longitude. At once the king set up a commission to look into St Pierre's proposals, a commission involving the talents of (among others) Christopher Wren, the physicist Robert Hooke, and Lord Brouncker, President of the Royal Society and Controller of the Navy. The commission reported to the king that (a) St Pierre's proposals were unworkable and (b) that there was still no way of finding longitude by lunar observations. Nevertheless, they argued that an observatory should be built, under royal patronage, specifically for mapping the heavens – to press on with the lunar method and so establish at least a workable way of fixing longitude at sea. The king, a believer in the importance of maritime trade and a supporter of scientific endeavours (the Royal Society was established under his patronage in 1662), concurred and signed a royal warrant in March 1675. John Flamsteed, already well known for his talents as an astronomer, was appointed the king's 'astronomical observator', and given an annual stipend from the Office of Ordnance of a stingy £100.

The only thing left to determine was the location of the new Royal Observatory, with Flamsteed as its principal occupant. Hyde Park and Chelsea, well within London, were canvassed. But Sir Christopher Wren (who had yet to begin work on his Royal Naval Hospital) suggested the site of the old Greenwich Castle – the Duke Humphrey Tower perched on top of Greenwich Hill, taken over by Henry VIII and demolished at some time in the 1660s. This had a number of advantages: it was already in a royal park, so the land was the king's to start with; it was away from the smoke of London – even then, likely to cause problems with pollution; but it was still easy to get at, by well-used road and river connections. Wren (who was himself elected Savilian Professor of Astronomy at Oxford University in 1661) drew up the plans, following a royal warrant which decreed that 'According to such plot and design as shall be given to you by

Our Trusty and well-beloved Sir Christopher Wren Knight, Our Surveyor General, of the place and site of the said Observatory, you cause the same to be fenced in, built and finished'. Flamsteed cast a horoscope to determine the most propitious time to start building, and laid the foundation stone himself on 10 August 1675.

Money, as ever in these matters, was tight. A budget of just £500 was set for the entire cost of the building, and as a consequence, large parts of it were built using second-hand materials to keep the cost down. The foundations of the old castle became the base of the Observatory. A gatehouse which had been demolished at the Tower of London was pressed into service to provide lead, wood and iron. Bricks were brought up from a fort at Tilbury. Wooden spars came courtesy of the Navy Board. Six hundred and ninety barrels of decayed gunpowder were sold off to a Mr Polycarpus Wharton, to pay for labour and sundry other necessaries. The whole project came in at £20 9s. 1d. over budget. Flamsteed moved his equipment in, along with two servants, and just over a year after the laying of the foundation stone, the first observations with the great sextant were made.

Wren later wrote, 'Wee built indeed an Observatory at Greenwich . . . it was for the Observator's habitation and a little for pompe.' There was a small kitchen in the basement, four small rooms – bedroom, study and so on – on the ground floor, and the wonderous Octagon Room. Originally – and poetically –

known as the Great Star Room, this establishes one of the fundamental values of the whole Royal Observatory: that small spaces can enclose tremendous things. There is a sense of purpose combined with a faultless sense of taste in the Octagon Room which you only find in buildings dedicated to a specific function – such as Wren's Sheldonian Theatre in Oxford, or Decimus Burton's Palm House at Kew Gardens, or even Lewis Cubitt's King's Cross Station. The Octagon Room has one of the few remaining original Wren interiors: chaste and functional, but with a beautiful plaster cornice of roses, coronets and acanthus leaves, surmounted by a little dome ornamented with leaves and spirals. And of course, there are the elegantly proportioned windows – extremely tall, to make space for the long telescopes used in the seventeenth century, and ranged round for the best observation of eclipses and comets, allowing a constant play of light and shade during the day. Here, Flamsteed would make his observations of the night sky and could work on the problem of whether or not the earth rotated at a constant speed by checking the time kept by the stars, against the time kept by the sun. By establishing that the earth rotated at an even rate (was 'isochronical', to use his word), he would then have a constant figure against which to begin the great task of mapping the heavens.

For this experiment he had the assistance of the two most accurate clocks in the world. Both were built by the great clockmaker Thomas Tompion, in 1676, and were not only good timekeepers, but needed winding no more than once a year.

Apart from the use of clever pinwheel escapements and the most exacting construction, much of their accuracy came from their enormously long pendulums. The longer the pendulum, the greater the accuracy, and at 13 feet, Tompion's two pendulums were so large that Wren probably had to design the room *around* them. They were fitted behind the wall panelling (behind a pair of portraits of Charles II and James I, in fact), and the pendulum bobs can still be seen through small inspection windows, swaying gently.

It took two months to install the clocks and get them going – after which they suffered the kind of teething troubles that all very new, very high-tech equipment is apt to experience. Lack of oil, temperature fluctuations, vibrations in the building, dirt and dust all caused the movements to run badly, or even to stop. Things were made worse by the fact that Tompion jealously refused to allow Flamsteed a key to the door behind which the clockwork was set so that he could make adjustments himself. Eventually, however, the clocks were successfully set up, and Flamsteed, in a rare moment of cheerfulness, wrote that 'Our clocks kept so good a correspondence with the heavens that I doubted not but they would prove the Revolutions of the earth to be Isochronicall . . .' Thus the first use of Greenwich Mean Time enabled him to prove (within the limits of the day; science has since modified his assumption) that the earth did revolve at a constant rate. From this he developed his 'Equation of Natural Days', recording the changing relationship between mean time and earth-sun time, which became the formula employed by every observatory in the world for the next two hundred years.

Things were not always this straightforward. The Astronomer Royal spent much of the rest of the time suffering from the vicissitudes of fate and the short-sightedness of his fellow men. Plagued by a frankly cantankerous disposition and chronic ill health (the migraines and fevers which afflicted him at Greenwich were not helped, one imagines, by the solitary, nocturnal life he was obliged to lead), he was also chronically poor. Not only did he have to provide his own instruments and pay for any skilled assistance he might need, but the cheapskate £100 per annum (plus £26 for an assistant) he received from the Office of Ordnance was so paltry that he had to take on paying pupils to make ends meet. As he once wrote to his patron, the mathematician and Surveyor-General of the Ordnance, Sir Jonas Moore (who apparently once rid himself of sciatica 'By boiling his buttock'): 'I must desire to be excused the trouble of them' – his private pupils – 'since you know very well I have work of another nature under my hands.' Elsewhere, he gamely vows (in a letter to the scientist Richard Towneley) to press on with his trials, provided that the Office of Ordnance does not 'Starve mee . . . out, for my allowance you know is but small and now they are 3 Quarters in my debt, I feare I must come downe to the country to seeke some poore vicarage, then farewell to our experiment . . .'

The rooms in Flamsteed House – restored with the same high-quality restraint that you find in the Queen's House – aptly suggest a modest, confined way of life. Two high-back Jacobean-style chairs and a richly coloured four-poster bed are about the only bits of furniture to hint at self-indulgence. Everything else, including the size and proportions of the rooms, is along the lines of a student's lodgings in an old Oxford or Cambridge college. The fact that the windows are kept shuttered, and the lights on, only adds to the sense of confinement as well as hinting at the sort of permanent dislocation with which Flamsteed lived, the building shuttered for sleep during the day, so that he could labour at night. When he was aged forty-six, he did at least find a companion for his loneliness, in the form of one Margaret Cooke, whom he married and who helped him in his studies as well as running his small household. Sir James Thornhill included a small portrait of Flamsteed – done from life – among the details of his ceiling in the Painted Hall of the Royal Naval Hospital: Flamsteed (seen with his doughty assistant, Abraham Sharp, gazing at him for inspiration and instruction) looks pretty run-down – stooping, his beaky nose cruelly accentuated by the dark rings around his eyes, his skin lugubriously sallow. He looks, in short, exhausted. Hardly surprising, since he had taken – with his principal instrument, a seven-foot mural sextant – 20,000 separate observations between 1676 and 1690, the first astronomer to use telescopic sights systematically for all his measurements.

Things looked up materially a little when he acquired the living of Burstow in Surrey (Flamsteed was ordained a clergyman in 1675) and also when his father died, leaving him a small inheritance. This promptly went on a new piece of equipment – a 10-foot wall-mounted quadrant, which cost £120 and fourteen months' work. Designed by the physicist Robert Hooke, this enabled Flamsteed to complete a further 28,000 observations before he died, even though he complained (yet again) that 'I tore my hands by it'. The sad thing is that neither the seven- nor the ten-foot quadrant went up in Wren's beautiful Octagon Room. This turned out to be no use for charting the heavens, as it was built slightly off the north–south meridian – the result of placing the Observatory directly on top of the foundations of Duke Humphrey's Tower, which was skewed slightly to the west. To map the stars as Flamsteed did, you have to fix a sighting instrument exactly on a north–south meridian, then record each star against that meridian as it appears to move across the sky, using a clock to measure the intervals of the earth's rotation. So Flamsteed built himself a shed at the bottom of the garden through which the meridian ran true, and spent the next forty-three years there with his sighting instruments, the roof shutters open and the night air gusting in. This, not – ironically enough – Wren's room, was the real heart of the Observatory.

Work proceeded slowly and painstakingly. Flamsteed saw himself as effectively beholden to no one, and resolved to publish his findings in his own time. He wanted his results to be as perfect as he could make them; and when Sir Isaac Newton started to exert pressure on him to publish (so that he could complete his own researches), Flamsteed dug his heels in. But without influential friends (and who, anyway, could face up to Sir Isaac Newton, a knight, President of the Royal Society, the pre-eminent scientist of his day?), Flamsteed was on his own.

Coerced by Newton, Queen Anne (Flamsteed's employer by this time) ordered that his observations should be published, whether he wanted them to be or not. The famous astronomer Edmond Halley, one of Flamsteed's most detested enemies, got the job of editing the material into book form, and in 1712 the *Historia Coelestis Britannica* came out, full of errors and abridgements and with only 97 pages incontrovertibly Flamsteed's own work. You can tell how strained relations were when you consider the manner in which the queen's representatives paid Flamsteed their only official visit, in 1713. Newton and Halley were both in the party: Flamsteed gave them a glass of wine – in the somewhat cramped hall of his home – and then left them to it, saying that the queen's officials could go wherever they liked in his Observatory, apart from his library. And those were the only words exchanged between them.

It was only when Flamsteed's fortunes in court improved, with George I's succession to the throne, that he could right some of the wrongs he felt had been done to him. He managed to get hold of 300 of the 400 copies of *Historia Coelestis Britannica* which had been printed, and burned them, 'as a sacrifice to heavenly truth'. It wasn't until 1725, some six years after his death, that his British catalogue of star positions was published as he would have wanted it – finished by his assistant, Abraham Sharp. It listed more stars – 3,000 of them – more accurately than any previous work; immediately it became the single most important text in the field, and even now some stars are still known by the numbers which his system allotted to them.

On Flamsteed's death, Edmond Halley took over the job of Astronomer Royal, and promptly added to the assembly of buildings which made up the Royal Observatory by building a new Quadrant Room and affixing a splendid new eight-foot iron mural quadrant to a newly built quadrant wall. Halley had already done much of his pioneering work by the time he became Astronomer Royal, but he did set himself the awesome task of observing the position of the moon whenever it crossed the meridian, over a period of eighteen years the so-called eclipse or saros cycle governing solar and lunar eclipses. He started in 1722, aged sixty-six, and died in 1742 at the age of eighty-six – just about meeting the challenge he set himself in his Greenwich Quadrant Room. The fact that many of his observations were inaccurate (Halley had an oddly casual approach to recording numbers) took the edge off his achievement; but it was still quite a way to end his career. Still, the new, north-facing quadrant was much praised at the time, its scaled markings in particular showing 'a degree of accuracy unknown before'. But it cost over £200, and once it had been put in, Halley ran out of money to buy a second, south-facing one.

He actually had more than one reason for installing this fancy new equipment: part of it was to do with the fact that Flamsteed's brick meridian wall was starting to subside downhill into the Royal Park – so a new wall would have to be built, a little further east; and part of it was due to the fact that on his death, Flamsteed's widow had vacated the Observatory, taking with her every last piece of scientific equipment, personal property and furniture that she could lay her hands on. The building was effectively a shell, as it had been when Flamsteed moved in, forty-odd years before.

With the arrival of the brilliant James Bradley as the third Astronomer Royal in 1742, things took another turn. Bradley was already celebrated for having provided empirical proof of Copernicus's theory that the earth revolved around the sun – first published some two hundred years earlier. He also discovered the phenomenon known as *nutation* – the tendency of the earth to wobble very slightly as it rotates on its axis. These two achievements alone were major steps forward in our understanding of the physical universe, and may have contributed to the fact that Bradley's wage was a relatively bearable £250 per annum; on top of which he was granted a massive £1,000 for the purchase of scientific instruments. Bradley built yet another room in which to make his observations – east of Halley's room –

equipped it with a splendid new eight-foot telescope lined up on his new meridian – and then found himself immortalised in a map-making experiment involving the British and the French.

In 1783, the French and British governments concluded that it would be a good idea to map the area between the meridian in Paris and the meridian in Greenwich and measure the distance between the Paris and Greenwich Observatories more accurately. For this, they used the method known as triangulation: this entails taking a measured baseline and establishing two adjacent angles with the aid of a theodolite, then working out mathematically the length of the two unknown sides, and so establishing the size of the whole triangle; which is then adjacent to another triangle, whose size you calculate, and so on, allowing distances and areas to be established on a grand scale. And which initial line was used on the British side? The Greenwich Meridian, established for his own use by Bradley, and which is still marked on the wooden floor of Bradley's Transit Room. What's more, this prime meridian, the longitude 0°, is *still* used on British Ordnance Survey maps – and has been used ever since the very first Ordnance Survey map (produced in response to France's busy map-making activities, and the by-product of Britain's being a militarily power-conscious national state), which covered the county of Kent and was published in 1801. This remained the official Prime Meridian of Great Britain until 1850, when Sir George Biddell Airy, the seventh Astronomer Royal, decided to build yet another platform for heavenly observation in the room next to Bradley's Transit Room. At which point, history was again made.

Airy was Astronomer Royal from 1835 to 1881. Lucasian Professor of Mathematics and Plumian Professor of Astronomy at Cambridge, he was not only a powerfully influential scientist, but also had a Victorian zeal for organisation and industry. He reorganised the workings of the Observatory, installed much new equipment, and saved countless observations from loss by neglect. Ever since the Observatory was built, in fact, it had been somehow marginal, while still being of crucial scientific importance to the state. For the first hundred and fifty years, the Astronomer Royal never had more than two assistants. One of these, a certain Thomas Evans, assistant to Nevil Maskelyne (Astronomer Royal from 1765 to 1811), actually wrote a despairing commentary on his working life: 'Nothing can exceed the tediousness and ennui of the life the assistant leads in this place, excluded from all society except, perhaps, that of a poor mouse . . .' As if that wasn't enough, he goes on in the same pitiful vein, 'Here, forlorn, he spends days, weeks, months in the same wearisome computations, without a friend to shorten the tedious hours, or a soul with which he can converse . . .'

How bad can it have been? Even now, even with the press of London all around it, the Observatory can be a surprisingly lonely place: everything else is so close by, and yet so hard to reach. As you turn away from the town of Greenwich below and look south towards the great rise of the Heath, you can catch a sense of how isolated it might sometimes have felt, with the footpads of eighteenth-century Blackheath in one direction and the friendly lights of Croom's Hill obscured by trees and the shape of the land in the other. With the shutters back in Bradley's Transit Room on a clear winter's night, it would also have been penetratingly cold and dark, with for company only an occasional owl flitting past, the lights of ships riding at anchor a mile below on the Thames, and the silent immensity of the galaxy.

John Pond, Astronomer Royal from 1811, was almost alarmingly frank about the qualities he looked for in a member of his team: 'I want indefatigable, hard-working, and, above all, obedient drudges (for so I must call them, although they are drudges of a superior order), men who will be contented to pass half their day in using their hands and eyes in the mechanical act of observing, and the remainder of it in the dull process of calculation.' Airy himself made a point of keeping the assistants' pay low, to put them off the idea of working permanently at the Observatory. Famously, he worked his assistants (by that time, the staff at the Observatory had swelled to well over twenty) enormously hard: up to twelve hours a day, churning out tremendous quantities of data. He was also a thoroughgoing obsessive, keeping exact notes (among other things) of how many times he cleaned his pens with blotting paper. But he did bring about a freshening of the pace at Greenwich, both by his administrative zeal and by the installation of a majestic new telescope, built on yet another new meridian: a piece of astronomical apparatus with global implications.

This was Airy's Great Transit Circle – a stunningly big refracting telescope built around an eight-inch lens which Airy bought in 1848. So unusual was this lens – the manufacture of an eight-inch lens in the mid-nineteenth century would have presented the maker with serious problems of weight and optical irregularities; a flawless one was something special – that he designed a huge permanent telescope around it. He installed it in a room built in 1809, adjacent to the Bradley Room, and there mounted the apparatus on a specially constructed brickwork base, with the telescope, like a large field gun, resting on mounts allowing it to swing through 360°. The operator sat in a whitewashed trench, just below ground level, resting on a hard wooden chair, while the telescope swivelled up towards whichever part of the north or south sky was due for observation. Even now, a century and a half later, it still strikes awe in the onlooker – especially after the smaller, more human proportions of Halley's and Bradley's telescopes. This is a device of a different order, the telescope and axis alone weighing 2,000 pounds, one which – as with any modern, professional astronomical telescope – has gone beyond the simple notion of a man applying his eye to a glass lens and peering at distant objects. It marks the point at which the technology had begun to dictate its own terms of size and complexity.

This physically daunting structure has a sequence of micrometer microscopes set on the western side around the axis. From these precision instruments, grouped in a ring around the centre of the axis and set into monumental base, the exact angle of elevation of the telescope can be read off, allowing the recorder to note any distortions as the telescope moves in its mounting: 'reading the circle', as it was known. The degree of accuracy of these micrometer readings was to within one hundredth of a second of an arc: or 360 thousandths of a degree. With this wonderful machine, Airy and his successors made more than 600,000 observations, and it was last officially used in 1954. Needless to say, being a piece of cherished Victorian engineering, it still works perfectly well today.

But the greatest legacy of Airy's Transit Circle is the line on which it is sited – the meridian on which he chose to locate the telescope, just a little to the east of Bradley's: the meridian which became the prime meridian of the world, the point at which the universal day begins, the beginning of the year 2000. It sounds like a God-given direction *Place the meridian here* or the result of some inescapable natural law; but in reality, it's the product of accident and historical forces.

As ever, longitude is behind it all. Abbreviating the story for now, we can simply consider the question, where do you put longitude 0° on the map? If the imaginary lines of longitude run from the North Pole to the South, and divide the earth up into 360 imaginary degrees, where do you start? Where do you put a line so that at any point of the globe you can fix your east–west position by working out how far you've travelled from your given starting point – a starting point, what's more, that's recognised by the rest of the world as the only one to apply, wherever you are? How do you pick a prime meridian? Obviously, you can put it anywhere you like, and for over two thousand years, this has been one of the key questions for navigators and map-makers.

Hipparchus, the Greek astronomer first had a go at fixing it on the island of Rhodes, where he was working at the time. Ptolemy, the Egyptian astronomer and geographer, then moved the prime meridian to the Canary Islands – the western edge of the known world. By the time of the Renaissance, increasing sea travel saw further attempts to fix a point. Pope Alexander VI tried to set it just west of the Cape Verde Islands; while Philip II of Spain moved the meridian to the city of Toledo. The sixteenth-century map-maker Mercator preferred to use the islands of the mid-Atlantic, while in the seventeenth century, Cardinal Richelieu called an international conference to settle the matter – with the westernmost of the Canary Isles coming out as the chosen spot. This was certainly adhered to by the French for the next hundred years; but for the rest of the world things went on much as before, each nation tending to use whatever prime meridian it felt like – often the capital city, or the site of its principal observatory. Navigators at sea didn't even attempt this, preferring to take their port of departure as 0° and counting east or west of that. In other words, if you examined a sea chart in the eighteenth century, the chances were that the principal point of longitude would depend entirely on what country the chart had been printed in.

Things only began to change significantly with Nevil Maskelyne's *Nautical Almanac* of 1767. At the time, the most reliable way for mariners to work out their longitude in the middle of a large and featureless ocean was to examine the positions of certain known heavenly bodies with an instrument such as a sextant, and then look up the results in a table giving the positions of moon and stars for any given date. They could then work out their position from the initial longitude used by the maker of the table. Well, Maskelyne's *Nautical Almanac* was the first reliable and practical almanac in the world, and – since Maskelyne was Astronomer Royal at the Greenwich Royal Observatory – it took the Greenwich Meridian as its starting point. Immediately, British navigators started to use it, alongside the British-made charts, which set longitude 0° at Greenwich. Other nations adopted the *Nautical Almanac*, as well, which meant that their charts had to have the same longitude arrangement as British ones. From the late eighteenth century onwards the British system began to be the world leader, the standard operating system, as it were. J. W. F. DesBarres produced a series of charts of the east coast of North America in 1784, and his too used the Greenwich Meridian – establishing it as conventional practice for the United States, and giving Greenwich a major boost. Even the Russians went over to Greenwich in the mid-nineteenth century, when the High Admiral of the Russian Fleet

threw out the nautical almanac which had been exclusively prepared for Russia and joined the majority. By the late 1800s, it was
estimated that 72 per cent of the world's shipping (on the basis of
tonnage) was using charts which had Greenwich as the prime
meridian; and 90 per cent of navigators involved in world trade
were doing likewise.

It was clear that some kind of agreement was needed to for-
malise the situation. A succession of international geographical
conferences was held, to thrash out the issue once and for all. For
over a decade, the argument about where to put the prime meridian, or whether simply to ratify the *de facto* Greenwich Meridian,
went backwards and forwards. The Great Pyramid at Giza was
promoted as an alternative, as were Jerusalem and the Bering
Straits. It was noted that, although Greenwich was the main
meridian for sea charts, land maps frequently used major cities for
0° longitude, and that while Japan and India may have had
Greenwich for both sea charts and land maps, Bavaria (with no
coastline) took Munich as the prime meridian for its maps; while
Holland used Amsterdam, Italy used Rome, and France used
Paris. Then the French suggested a trade-off with the British: if
the French were to accept Greenwich as the prime meridian,
would the British reciprocate by going over to the metric system?
Even Airy himself perversely tried to put a spanner in the works.
'If a Prime Meridian were to be adopted,' he wrote, 'it must be
that of Greenwich, for the navigation of almost the whole world
depends on calculations founded on that of Greenwich.' So far,

so good. But then he continues, 'But I as Superintendent of the Greenwich Observatory, entirely repudiate the idea of founding any claim on this: Let Greenwich do her best to maintain her high position in administering to the longitude of the world, and Nautical Almanacs do their best, and we will unite our efforts without special claim to the fictitious honour of a Prime Meridian.'

True Victorian confidence – but it didn't make any difference to the final outcome, which was decided at the International Meridian Conference, held in Washington, DC, in 1884. The United States offered to host the conference, as it had 'the greatest longitudinal extension of any country traversed by railway and telegraph lines', and in due course forty-one delegates from twenty-five countries arrived in Washington, in October. A month of wrangling and voting later, and the key questions had been answered. All the countries had voted in favour of the principle of a single prime meridian (apart from a handful who weren't present – Denmark, for instance, never made it to Washington). Twenty-two out of twenty-five voted for Greenwich as the prime meridian (Brazil and France abstained; San Domingo voted against). Twenty-three out of twenty-five voted in favour of the principle of the universal day, beginning at the prime meridian – the precise wording being that the universal day is 'to begin for all the world at the moment of mean midnight of the initial meridian'. And with a vote of fourteen to five, with six abstaining, it was agreed that longitude should be counted in two directions up to 180°, east longitude being plus and west longitude minus.

And where would the fixed point be set? Where, *exactly*, was the prime meridian on which all this was to hinge? It was 'the centre of the Transit Instrument at the Observatory at Greenwich', the absolute centre of the cross-hairs of Airy's 1850 device, repeated in the form of the brass strip which runs across the floor and out into the courtyard. This is longitude 0°, and on one side is the western hemisphere of the world; on the other is the eastern. You can – and most people do – bestride the brass strip and stand with a foot in both hemispheres, almost as if this were the only place in the world where such a thing is possible. But of course, longitude 0° describes an imaginary line from pole to pole, so you could also stand on a spot just outside Le Mans, in northern France, or near the town of Caspe, in north-eastern Spain, or stand in the western Sahara, or even watch your GPS navigation system flip over as you sail east to west in the southern Atlantic. All these would mark the prime meridian just as well.

Except that Greenwich created it: if Henry VII hadn't taken a liking to Placentia, if Henry VIII hadn't developed it, if Greenwich Park hadn't been enclosed as a royal park, if Charles II hadn't been persuaded to use that patch of free land for the Observatory he wanted, and if Nevil Maskelyne the Astronomer Royal hadn't produced his *Nautical Almanac* when he did, then longitude 0° could now be in Paris, or Madrid or Washington, or possibly (as Willem Blaeu, the seventeenth-century cartographer decided) on the highest point of the island of Tenerife. But Greenwich is where it all starts.

After this, anything else astronomical might seem very slightly anticlimatic. Not so far as the astronomers were concerned, though. No sooner had Airy started taking observations with his Great Transit Circle than work began on a new building, designed to house a larger telescope. This was the Great Equatorial Building, just to the east of the old Royal Observatory. Finished in 1857, it was home to a Munich-built refracting telescope with a lens of nearly 13 inches diameter, which subsequently made way in 1893 for an even larger refracting telescope – one with a 28-inch lens which alone weighed 225 pounds – still the biggest in Britain, the seventh largest in the world, and getting close to the limits for refracting telescopes (a limit currently reached by the 40-inch refracting telescope at the Yerkes Observatory, Wisconsin). The massive revolving, pivoting structure of Airy's second telescope – the whole thing weighing one and a half tons – had to be housed in a larger, onion-dome roof fixed to the old base. The original onion dome was made of steel and papier mâché; the one we can see is fibreglass, and was put on in 1975.

Shortly after that, the Planetarium – or South Building, as it was originally known – was constructed, just a little way off. Its function was to house two large telescopes and provide some administrative space for the Observatory staff. Since 1967, though, it's been a planetarium rather than an observatory – a creator of images rather than an observer of nature. Easily overlooked in the general crush to explore the Old Observatory, it's still a wonderful building in its own right: covered in furiously busy, baroque red terracotta, with the names of the great astronomers carved above the windows and a weather vane in the form of a four-masted sailing ship, it loiters in a slightly overweight, awkward manner behind Wren's little jewel of a building and its unassuming Georgian additions, like a large Victorian dowager hoping to attract one's attention.

It is also the last significant building to be put up here, on the summit of Greenwich Hill. The twentieth century not only brought all kinds of changes to the maritime centres of Greenwich, Deptford and Woolwich, down below; it also saw the gradual end of the Observatory's work. The new power station on the waterfront plus the electrification of the local railway network started to interfere with the astronomers' sensitive magnetic equipment. Light pollution and smog hampered the visual observations of the telescopes. During the Second World War the department responsible for the *Nautical Almanac* (which was still going strong, nearly two hundred years after Maskelyne's first edition) was moved out of the way of bombing, and relocated in Bath. And in 1946 it was decided to leave London altogether and re-establish the Observatory at Herstmonceux Castle in Sussex. The Astronomer Royal of the day (Sir Harold

Spencer Jones) left Greenwich in 1948, and the last positional observations were taken in May 1954.

(But then, purely in parenthesis – was the South Building really the last significant building to join the historic Observatory group? Well, yes and no: quite apart from all the repairs and restorations needed after the Observatory moved to Herstmonceux – there was still bomb damage left behind from the war – and again, in the second major refurbishment in the early 1990s, there was one part of the institution in the group which managed to re-dedicate itself to a purpose it had previously lost sight of. This was the Camera Obscura. When the Old Observatory was first completed in 1676, it looked much as it does today: Wren's delicate grouping of the tall windows, the small balcony beneath the middle north-facing window of the Octagon Room, the two small towers, and the delightful scrolled volutes bracketing the north façade, has barely changed over the centuries. What you wouldn't have seen in 1676 were the time-ball – which dates from the nineteenth century – and, in all probability, the two little buildings on either side of the north façade. Now known as the eastern and western Summerhouses, it seems that Wren added them after the main building was completed, possibly to give a final balance to the overall composition. But once the eastern Summerhouse had been added on, Flamsteed at once took it over for a specific purpose: he installed a camera obscura inside.

So what was this camera obscura? Essentially it was a kind of microscope, mounted in a swivelling ball mechanism, with one end looking up at the sky, the other projecting whatever images it picked up on to a flat screen, about the size of a large book. With it, Flamsteed could safely observe sun spots and solar eclipses, and with the help of the ball mechanism he could track the sun as it moved across the sky. He noted with some satisfaction in 1684, 'I observed the eclipse of the Sun . . . on a screen in a darkened room.' Indeed, by the time the German scholar Uffenbach came to visit Flamsteed early in the eighteenth century, there were two cameras obscura, probably in the little turrets on top of the Octagon Room – the view from which the German scholar Zacharius Uffenbach was moved to coin his remark about 'the charming prospect and the great traffic on the Thames'.

When Flamsteed died, of course, Mrs Flamsteed extracted all of his possessions, including whatever cameras obscura he may have installed, and that seems to have been that, until the arrival of Nevil Maskelyne in 1765. Following Flamsteed's example, he put a camera obscura in the western turret above the Octagon Room for the purpose of observing the sun; a pretty watercolour by his daughter, Margaret, clearly depicts the little drum on the roof of the turret which houses the camera's mechanism. This device stayed put until 1840, when Sir George Biddell Airy had it taken out and an anemometer put in its place. And that was the last camera obscura at Greenwich – until 1994, and the second big restoration programme. It was decided to reinstate a camera obscura in the eastern Summerhouse, the home of Flamsteed's original camera – but to make it, instead of a specialist tool for viewing the sun, a reproduction of a nineteenth-century tourist attraction. This type of camera obscura was – before the arrival of cinema – an enormously popular way of displaying moving images. A darkened booth would be fitted out with a white table, a rotating mirror system and a type of lens known as a meniscus lens. The mirror would reflect whatever was going on outside the booth, through the lens, which then focused it on to the table, round which a group of people would congregate to enjoy the spectacle. There were portable, roving cameras obscura; temporary ones at holiday resorts; permanent ones in Edinburgh, Aberystwyth and Bristol.

The pleasure derived from watching a colour image of the moving world outside must have been peculiarly subtle and intense – as it is nowadays, in the new Greenwich Camera Obscura. In a world in which we can watch huge IMAX screens, be deafened with quad sound and have animatronic monsters jump out at us in theme park rides, the idea of getting pleasure from standing in a small, darkened room, spying on the world outside, seems not only old hat, but positively bizarre. Yet it's entirely engrossing, whimsical and funny: a simple entertainment after the serious matters of Observatory history. Even Flamsteed might have smiled.

SCIENTIFIC II

AND THEN there is still the problem of longitude. In 1714, nearly thirty years after the appointment of the first Astronomer Royal, Sir Isaac Newton reported to a House of Commons committee that the situation was still capable of improvement and that current thinking provided four possible solutions.

The first was the clock solution. You could work out longitude by using an extremely accurate clock: every mile you go to east or west, you lose or gain time in relation to the point at which you started (as all air travellers now take for granted, when they fly across the Atlantic). If you had one absolutely reliable clock on board, permanently set to the time of your home port; and another – less reliable – one which you re-set every day to read noon when the sun was at its height (easy enough to do, with a sextant), then the difference between the two clocks would show how far east or west you had travelled. Unfortunately, in 1714 no clock in the world could withstand life at sea and keep really accurate time. Clocks were generally pendulum contraptions, and the rolling of the boat would upset the motion of the pendulum; to say nothing of the changes in temperature, and the invasion of damp, which would foul up the clock's mechanism, pendulum or no. So that solution – easily the best and most elegant of the four – was still awaiting the development of a workable, accurate ship's timepiece.

Second, was to observe the eclipses of the satellites of Jupiter. This was practicable on land, where you could set up the large telescopes necessary for the observations; and where the ground stayed still while you observed. On a ship there wasn't enough space for the astronomical instruments, and even if there had been, all the rolling and pitching would make it impossible to take a decent sighting.

Third, was to use the position of the moon in the night sky, fixing longitude by lunar observations – the principle behind Astronomer Royal Flamsteed's *Historia Coelestis Britannica*. This was possible, still an ongoing project, and a real improvement on what had gone before; but it was only accurate to within two or three degrees of longitude, when for real safety one degree of variation was all that was permissible.

Fourth – and state of the art – was a plan put forward by two mathematicians, William Whiston and Humphrey Ditton. They argued that the best way forward was to use the known trade routes, and to moor – at fixed, known, positions along these routes – signal ships, which would fire enormous rockets or flares precisely at midnight their time. Ships at sea would have to keep roughly within range of one of the signal ships, keep a watch specifically to spot the signal rocket, and then use a compass bearing to determine the ship's direction from the signal ship, and thus how closely it was sticking to the trade route. All OK in theory, but if a ship sailed out of range of the signal vessels (assuming that they could be satisfactorily fixed – and Whiston and Ditton massively underestimated the depth of the Atlantic and thus how long the anchor chains would have to be), how could it re-establish its position? And if a ship could sail only via the set trade routes, how much more time and effort would it take to manoeuvre from one route to another, just to get to its destination?

All in all, it was not a promising outlook. So it was with a sense of real urgency that the British government pushed through its Longitude Act of 1714, establishing a Board of Longitude and challenging the scientific community to find an improved method of calculating longitude anywhere in the world. A maximum prize of £20,000 – several millions in today's terms – was the bait for the most accurate method devised: which meant to within half a degree.

Apart from Whiston and Ditton's scheme, there were other

fervently argued proposals. Perpetual motion machines held in giant vacuum bottles was one; while the most notorious was probably the Powder of Sympathy. Back in the seventeenth century, Sir Kenelm Digby ('the handsomest gentleman in England', his portrait hangs in the Queen's Antechamber of the Queen's House) claimed to have discovered a powder which, when placed in contact with a knife that had wounded someone, would instantaneously cause the victim to feel the pain just as sharply as when the original injury was inflicted. The scheme? To amass a supply of Kenelm Digby's Powder of Sympathy; to wound a large number of dogs with the same knife; put the dogs on board ships bound for destinations all over the globe; and then, at midday at Greenwich (midday being reasonably easy to ascertain on dry land), stick the knife into a jar of Powder of Sympathy, thus causing all the wounded dogs, wherever they were, to yelp and howl as if feeling the wound all over again. In this way the ship's crew could set whatever clock they had to Greenwich noon, compare this with a second clock, set to local noon by the sun, and work out their longitude.

The reliable sea clock was clearly still the best – but apparently unrealisable – idea. It took a mechanical genius called John Harrison to make it a reality.

Harrison's story has been well told elsewhere. A much-abbreviated version runs like this. The self-taught son of a Lincolnshire village carpenter, Harrison early on developed a fascination with clockmaking. In his thirties he came to London, befriended the Astronomer Royal, Edmond Halley, at Greenwich, and was introduced to a Mr George Graham of London, then the greatest clockmaker of the day. Graham was enormously impressed by Harrison's ideas for a sea-clock and provided the funds for him to build it. This clock became known as H1, worked brilliantly, and won the admiration of the scientific community. But Harrison, a stickler for perfection, was dissatisfied. He persuaded the Board of Longitude to advance him £250 and started work on an improved version, H2, soon abandoning it when he realised that it contained certain fundamental flaws. He then started on H3 and spent the next nineteen years obsessively perfecting this machine, before a realisation struck him: the three machines he had spent the last twenty-seven years of his life working on were all big, heavy, frighteningly complex clocks. What was needed was something much smaller, a large watch, in fact: the small, high-frequency oscillator at the heart of the watch mechanism would be a much more dependable timekeeper. This became H4. It looks like an oversized silver pocket watch (weighing a hefty three and a bit pounds) and has a claim to be the most important timekeeper ever made. It failed its first sea trial, but in 1763 it was given a second trial, being sent to Barbados for the purpose. It performed three times better than the minimum rate set by the Longitude Act, could be copied, and was clearly the answer to the dilemma which had been plaguing navigators since sailing began.

There was only one snag. Nevil Maskelyne was about to become Astronomer Royal. And Maskelyne – with the publication of his *Nautical Almanac* looming – was a fierce proponent of the 'lunar distance' method of determining longitude; a method which had been given an important boost by the publication of Tobias Meyer's new, improved lunar tables and the development of the highly accurate reflecting quadrant (precursor of the sextant) by inventor John Hadley. Combining the rigorous and extensive information contained in the *Nautical Almanac* with the new, precise reflecting quadrant would mean that a reasonably skilled navigator at sea could use the positions of the stars to calculate the time back at Greenwich and compare it with the time on board ship, with a fair degree of accuracy. Overall, the amount of time and effort involved would be reduced from four hours to half an hour. Harrison's clocks may potentially have been better – and were certainly less complex to use – but Maskelyne wanted the title of 'The Man Who Discovered Longitude' for himself. And being set in judgement over Harrison (he went, for instance, to Barbados in 1673 to set up an observatory with which to check the watch's performance) it was clear that Maskelyne, with all the resources of the establishment behind him, was not going to give in to the provincial loner, Harrison. So Harrison went through years of torment with H4, the perfect watch, subsequently using a copy known as H5 to continue the fight, as the government refused to pay the prize money and then retrospectively changed the rules of the competition (it ended up that all timekeepers had to be made in duplicate, then tested for a year at Greenwich, followed by two sea trips around Great Britain, then anywhere in the world the Board of Longitude might name, finishing up with a final year's examination back at Greenwich). Finally, Harrison appealed to the king, George III, and in 1773 at last got the prize money owing to him. He died in 1776, aged eighty-three, his whole working life spent in the perfection of this handful of mechanical timepieces.

And there they are, in the Royal Observatory. But you really need to know something of their history in order to appreciate the gravity which hangs about them. Otherwise, Harrison's inventions (especially the epoch-making H4) look old and odd and ingenious, but not earth-shattering. H1 is definitely the strangest, with its spheres and springs and weird levers. It weighs 75 pounds and had to be transported on its sea trials in a specially designed case – yet its extravagant cleverness is such that William Hogarth, a keen amateur of timekeepers, called it 'one of the most exquisite movements ever made'. H2 looks much more businesslike; and H3 – the one Harrison called 'My curious third machine', and which he never got right – even more so. But all them, however beautiful, however fascinating, with their glittering engraved faces and curious insect-like internal movements (Harrison called his friction-free escapement design the 'grasshopper'), lack the apparently simple robust integrity of

H4. So why isn't H4 kept going? Because it was designed to need regular servicing, lubrication and maintenance and would have to be completely dismantled every three years or so, to keep it in good condition. But as any horologist will point out, every time that happened, H4 couldn't help but be put back together in a slightly different way from that in which Harrison did it. The lubricating oil would degrade, very slightly; the tiny parts would inevitably wear; and it wouldn't be long before its character changed just enough for it not to be Harrison's watch any more. It has, in the world of timekeeping, the status of a sacred relic.

But after Harrison? Once he had cracked the problem of accurately determining longitude by means of a timekeeper (or chronometer, as it came to be known), the job arose of making watches as good as H4, but at a fraction of the price. John Arnold and Thomas Earnshaw were his immediate successors. Arnold managed to simplify the mechanics of late eighteenth-century timepieces; while Earnshaw used ruthless quality control and modern manufacturing techniques to turn them out in large numbers. A chronometer which cost £500 a few years earlier, was being sold at the end of the century for a mere 60 guineas or so. And where were they tested? At Greenwich. In 1821 the Admiralty instituted the testing of timekeepers. Any manufacturer who wanted the Navy's business had to submit his product to the Greenwich Observatory for a period of up to twelve months. During this time, his chronometer would – among other things – be shaken, steeped in water and heated in an oven at 38°C for several days. If it passed these tests and still kept time, then it became a candidate. And so, as man's ingenuity gradually brought time under control, Greenwich became more and more a centre for terrestrial timekeeping as well as celestial observation.

The next step was to provide a way to let nearby ships know what the time was ashore, without their having to work it out from first principles. This was becoming conventional practice anyway – guns were fired at specific times of day in coastal ports, or rockets fired, or flags dipped: anything that could easily be read by ships at sea and that would give them a clear idea of the time so that they could reset their ships' clocks. So in 1833 it was decided to equip the eastern turret of Flamsteed House with a mechanical time-ball, which would drop on the dot of 1 p.m. (not midday, because the crews would doubtless be working out their own calculations from the noonday sun at that time, time-ball or not) and so give the traffic in the Thames a reliable temporal point to work from. The first ball was covered in leather, and blew down in a gale in 1855. It was put back up, but replaced early in the twentieth century with a smart new aluminium one. It was, of course, more than just a convenience for passing vessels: it was almost certainly the world's first public time signal.

By the mid-nineteenth century Greenwich and time were synonymous. Naval almanacs and sea charts took Greenwich as the prime meridian; vessels sailing from British shores used Greenwich Mean Time as the basic starting point from which everything else sprang, and so, eventually, did the country as a whole – even though, when it's noon in London, it's (in strictly temporal terms) five past twelve in Norwich, a quarter to twelve at Plymouth and twenty minutes to twelve up on Ben Nevis.

Greenwich Mean Time is the one time used throughout the UK, no matter what regional variations there may be. But this didn't come about as a result of any kind of all-seeing plan: it arose with the growth of the railways, and the need for railway companies to standardise their timetables. Until the middle of the century it was still possible for a train to travel north to Manchester from London using London time; and then back south, using Manchester time. Just as when you get off the plane after any flight of much more than an hour, you find yourself adjusting your watch to the local time, so the passenger from the south had to set his watch to northern time to make sure he didn't miss the train back. The watchmaker Benjamin Lewis Vulliamy actually made a pocket watch in the mid-1800s which had two independently set minute hands – one for Greenwich Mean Time, the other for UK local time.

To avoid this asininity, the railway companies, one by one, made London time – or rather Greenwich time, since Greenwich is technically a good half-minute ahead of, say, Buckingham Palace – the only time in use on their schedules. Out in the provinces this was apt to be derided as 'railway aggression', some kind of plot by big business and London's city slickers to subjugate the liberties of the rest of the nation. But by 1855, 98 per cent of public clocks in Britain were showing Greenwich Mean Time. And so Greenwich found itself supplying the time not only to London's clockmakers (a service it had begun in 1836, when an assistant had to physically carry a watch, set at Greenwich, round the chronometer workshops of London), but also to the Post Office and the railways.

It was hardly something that the Observatory and its staff had intended, but events had overtaken them and they rose to the challenge. Indeed, Sir George Biddell Airy held the firm belief that Greenwich not only could but should provide Greenwich time whenever and wherever it was needed. He worked out a plan to synchronise all the clocks in the Observatory, and to distribute this same synchronous time, via telegraph wires, all over Britain and to those foreign observatories that requested it. This needed a new, electric master clock, which arrived in 1852: the product of Charles Shepherd of London, it cost £70. This was then linked in with 'slave' clocks around the Observatory complex (including the beautiful Shepherd twenty-four-hour clock by the main gates, the first clock to show Greenwich time to the public), and then by electric telegraph to a time-ball in the Strand, to a clock at London Bridge terminus, and throughout the rest of the country, following the distribution system run by the Electric Telegraph Company.

Greenwich Mean Time was now a matter of speed and precision. Not only did the signals from the master clock travel instantaneously down miles of electric cable; but the master clock itself was regulated by the most accurate timekeeping system then known – the stars. The routine for setting the master clock at Greenwich was this: calculate the time – every night, weather permitting – by observing the positions of certain bright stars (known as the 'clock stars'), using the Transit Circle; correct the Observatory clock; send out the time signal, every hour, on the hour; do the same again the next day, and so on – a regime which lasted well into the twentieth century, and whose fundamental principle, that the rotating earth is the best timekeeper, held good until atomic clocks started to gain currency in the 1960s and provide a time source even more reliable than the turning earth.

Despite all these marvellous advances, Greenwich Mean Time only became the *legal* time throughout Britain – the time at which details are recorded, reported crimes are committed or legal obligations become enforceable – after an Act of Parliament was passed in 1880. But well before then, the British public had got used to the idea of a single, reliable source of time regulating most aspects of their lives. As Airy himself piously pronounced, in 1865, 'I have indeed always considered it a very proper duty of the National Observatory to promote by utilitarian aid the dissemination of a knowledge of accurate time which is now really a matter of very great importance. The practical result of the system will be acknowledged by all those who have travelled abroad. We can, on an English railway, always obtain correct time, but not so on a French or German railway, where the clocks are often considerably in error.'

And there, in the Observatory Museum, the original electric master clock stands on view in its handsome wooden case, its carved scrolls reminding you of exactly how Victorian this device is, and at the same time visually complementing the coils of wires inside the cabinet – the last word in mid-nineteenth-century technological advancement. A 'slave' clock waits blankly beside the master, and this is where all the time in Britain – and, indeed, the world – once came from.

Of course, the Museum has a much smaller and more narrowly focused collection of timepieces than, say, the British Museum, whose horological department is one of the finest in the world, with an unbelievable assortment of rare, beautiful and important clocks. In comparison, the one at Greenwich is almost a private collection: indeed, some of the more playful items – the little French sundial which uses a burning-glass to fire off a miniature cannon at midday; the rolling-ball clock, designed and patented at Woolwich Royal Arsenal and capable of gaining or losing as much as half an hour every day – are really *jeux d'esprit* rather than serious horological trophies. But the other clocks, the Harrisons, the Observatory clocks and their successors and relations, the atomic clocks, the Russian-made pendulum clock of

1960 – the most accurate pendulum clock ever made, a wonderful (and dependable) anachronism from a time when the mechanical pendulum was disappearing – even their distant cousins, the navigational devices, astrolabes and quadrants, are all so charged with significance that the overall effect is potent. This is where some of the finest minds in the history of Western civilisation came together to make sense of the physical universe and bring a man-made order to the world we inhabit.

And what was true for Britain – this time regime based on a single clock at Greenwich – soon became globally applicable when the International Meridian Conference of 1884 brought in the universal day, beginning at mean midnight at Greenwich and divided into time zones based on the Greenwich Meridian. Not that adoption of GMT worldwide was any smoother than the adoption of GMT nationally: France held out against formal adoption of the system until 1911, Finland waited until 1921, the USSR until 1924, Holland only accepted it in 1940, and Saudi Arabia put it off until 1962. But it did happen, ultimately; and now it's hard to imagine anything different taking its place.

Meanwhile, a low-key debate was going on in the early years of the twentieth century, as to whether or not to transmit the Greenwich time signal by radio, rather than by telegraphic wire. The main beneficiary of this, it was thought, would be Britain's shipping, which wouldn't have to be within sight of a port with a Greenwich-controlled time-ball – such as Deal, or

Portsmouth – in order to get an accurate fix on the time. Curiously enough, the authorities were indifferent, arguing that time-balls in various ports, wherever they were, would be good enough, and, failing that, foreign-broadcast time signals – from France, Germany, the United States – would do. All that Greenwich was prepared to do about it was to install a wireless room in the Observatory to pick up foreign time signals, check them against the correct time at Greenwich and report any discrepancies to the foreign observatory responsible for the signal. It took another Astronomer Royal, Sir Frank Dyson, to sell the idea of a broadcast GMT signal to the BBC, in the 1920s. So the Great British public first listened to the Greenwich time signal – as expressed by Big Ben and broadcast on the BBC wireless – at the stroke of midnight, New Year's Eve, 1923. The following year, the six-pip time signal became a permanent feature of the BBC's output; twelve years on, and the Speaking Clock service began for telephone users, again taking its cue from Greenwich. Thus were two national institutions born.

Just as the Observatory was forced to change as the century wore on, so the timekeeping duties of Greenwich gradually evolved and had to move elsewhere. Ever since 1919, the job of co-ordinating and standardising the time signals generated by learned institutions all over the world (Greenwich was definitely not alone by now), had fallen to the Bureau International de l'Heure (BIH), in Paris; from which, ultimately, came what's known as Universal Time Co-ordinated, or UTC. The BIH then gave over its task to the Bureau International des Poids et Mesures, just outside Paris, which nowadays takes readings from over 200 atomic clocks in thirty-eight laboratories worldwide and extracts from them a single 'Mean clock' for the world. The BBC no longer uses Greenwich-originated pips for its time signal, instead using GPS satellite signals and the special radio signal broadcast from a 60 kHz transmitter at Rugby (this also keeps the time for personal radio signal clocks and wrist-watches) to generate its own time signal. Indeed, the national Greenwich time service stopped coming from Greenwich itself in 1940, when the war forced it to move down to Surrey. So what with one thing and another, the Greenwich Observatory, having pioneered so much, has finally called it a day, spread itself and its functions around the country – to Edinburgh, Cambridge, the National Physical Laboratory in Teddington – and across the world, with most of the astronomical observations taken at the Northern Hemisphere Observatory on the Island of La Palma, in the Canaries – definitively well away from the grime of London.

What remains is a wonderful relic – one of the most important buildings in Britain; one of the most significant buildings in the world, whose prime meridian and whose GMT (effectively the same as UTC) still stand – but one which is so quiet, so self-effacing, so much concerned with the cosmological vastness of creation and the minutiae which build it up, that it has no time for pomposity or fatuous grandeur. Just like the clocks and watches and astrolabes in its collection, small things contain tremendous meanings; or, as Christopher Marlowe once put it, 'So enclose Infinite riches in a little room'.

DOME

You CAN'T miss it. Whether you're coming into Docklands on the Docklands Light Railway; or looking west up the Thames, past Woolwich Reach and the Thames Barrier; or standing on the crown of Charlton Village – there it is: a bizarre, unearthly shape of twelve latticed yellow pylons sticking up into the sky, a web of cabling catching the light, and a great arc of grey-white stretching across the ground, its low mushroom shape answering the blunt point of Canary Wharf across the river. We now have the Dome, and yet again Greenwich has been dragged to the front of the national consciousness in a way that no one could possibly have foreseen.

But first, some facts. The Dome – indeed, the whole Millennium project – generates facts about itself the way a factory turns out tin cans. It looks vast, because it is: the largest structure of its kind in the world, it covers 20 acres and is big enough to hold two entire Wembley Stadiums or a total of thirteen Royal Albert Halls. It's been designed to cope with twelve million visitors in the first year of its life, or 30,000 visitors every day. It's two-thirds of a mile around the perimeter of the Dome (taking fifteen minutes just to walk around it), and the structure covers an area of 96,000 square yards. Nearly forty-four miles of cabling have gone into the roof, and the roof panelling sections cover one million square feet. It contains the UK's largest ever water conservation and recycling system, using recycled water to flush the six hundred and fifty-odd lavatories in the Dome. Twelve thousand trees have been planted across the site . . .

And the statistics spill over into the surrounding infrastructure – the new extension to the London Underground's Jubilee Line at the North Greenwich Transport Interchange is the largest underground station in Europe, capable of handling well over 50,000 passengers an hour, with parking space for up to a thousand cars. The Docklands Light Railway has been extended right under the river and down – via the *Cutty Sark* – into Lewisham, putting an extra half a million people within the DLR's catchment. Even the riverboats – the Cinderellas of London's passenger transport system, the neglected descendants of all those steamers and ferryboats of generations ago – have been given a lift, with the commissioning of £5 million worth of new, 500-seat riverboats, plus a new Millennium Pier able to take more than a million passengers a year. The Millennium Village will have over a thousand homes in it, all designed to use 80 per cent less energy than their late twentieth-century equivalents . . . and so it goes on. This is one of those rare endeavours which is on such a scale, and which involves so many people, that even its most mundane aspects become charged with significance.

Purists have, of course, pointed out that technically the Dome is not really a dome at all. Strictly speaking, an architectural dome sits on a base, exerting its thrust all around its perimeter – which is why the earliest domes in India and the Middle East had to have immensely thick supporting walls. Brunelleschi's beautiful and audacious fifteenth-century dome for the cathedral of Santa Maria del Fiore in Florence is a masterpiece, a landmark in architecture and engineering: double-skinned, daringly constructed – and also fantastically heavy. Brunelleschi had to devote endless time and energy to solving the various problems of keeping the dome from squashing itself under its own weight. Two hundred and fifty years later, Wren's dome for St Paul's Cathedral came about as the result of complex mathematical equations establishing precisely the right shape for the dome, so that it could support the various structures and adornments planned for it. And like Brunelleschi's dome, it couldn't stay up without iron bracing running around it, holding the structure together. *These*, some purists might argue, are *real* domes. The Dome at Greenwich, they would say, is a fancy tent. But the anti-purists might argue that domes have been changing their character for years, as new building techniques have arrived – steel, glass, moulded concrete forms, geodesic domes made of plastic; and that the most important part of a dome is less its engineering logic than whether or not it looks dome-shaped.

But then the Greenwich Dome introduces yet another definition into the argument. Not only is it much more like a smoothly geometric tent, held up by rigging wires and elaborate stays; it also has these twelve extremely visible pylons to hold it up, making it another kind of shape again – a domed crown, perhaps, with the pylons like the points on a nobleman's coronet, or the sort of crown Prince Charles wore for his investiture as Prince of Wales. And for the last few years Londoners have been living with these pylons, or masts, watching them rise from the ground, and using them to mark the passage of time and the gradual progress towards the millennium.

Not that everything went Greenwich's way to begin with. Back in the mid-1990s there was no consensus as to where to put the Millennium Exhibition, as it was being called then. The Greenwich Peninsula where the Dome now stands had been earmarked for development as something called Port Greenwich, and faced competition from a number of other sites around the country. There was, for instance, Pride Park, in Derby – which was a long shot however you looked at it, even though its backers were quite serious about it. Much the same could be said of a bid for the exhibition from the East London Meridian Site in Stratford, cunningly more or less on the Meridian, but on the other side of the river in an area mostly known for its railway yards and its pointed absence of historical charm.

Birmingham, on the other hand, was a real rival, and by the beginning of 1996 the competition for the millennium's number one spot in the UK had come down to the National Exhibition Centre on the edge of Birmingham; and Greenwich. Birmingham had a number of things going for it: not only the NEC complex itself, but also a large, greenfield site, all ready to go and needing no great work to bring it up to standard. The NEC, the ninth-biggest exhibition centre in Europe, had years of experience in promoting and staging world-class events; it was in the geographical heart of the UK, with more than thirty million people living less than two hours away; and it had excellent road and rail links. National Opinion Poll ran a survey among the marketing directors of the top 100 businesses in the UK and found that 60 per cent of them favoured Birmingham for the Millennium Exhibition.

Greenwich, on the other hand, was burdened with problems. For a start, communications were dismal – not just with the rest of the world, but with the rest of London. A single railway station with services into Charing Cross and Waterloo was the main way of getting in and out of town, with a few buses slogging along through Lewisham and New Cross. You could get the DLR down to Island Gardens and walk through the Foot Tunnel, but you really had to be motivated to find the time for all that. And if you were coming in from elsewhere – well, arriving at Waterloo via the Channel Tunnel, was a start; but flying in to Gatwick or Heathrow would mean a whole day fighting across town. And there was – and is – nowhere to park, nowhere to drive. On top of that (said the promoters of Birmingham, just to drive home their point), the National Lottery grant that was to prime all the subsequent Millennium Exhibition developments should be kept well away from London – which had already eaten up hundreds of millions of pounds of Lottery cash, depriving the rest of the country of what was meant to be a national resource. Don't, they said, give the capital any more. And to cap it all, there was the whole bitter question of the gasworks.

In 1886 the Metropolitan Gas Company opened the largest gasworks in Europe, on the Greenwich Peninsula. This huge enterprise not only had its own internal railway system (connecting with the Angerstein branch line) but had also put up the biggest gasholder in the world in the same year, followed by an even bigger one in 1891. In fact the earlier gasholder is still there, just under 200 feet high, a nicely old-fashioned industrial contrast to the smooth post-modern skin of the Dome. Chemical works soon made their way on to the site (while down in Woolwich, the Metropolitan Gas Company's fine showrooms concealed the murky origins of gas lighting in a palace of brackets, brasswork and glass), adding to the chemical haze which hung over the place and seeped into the ground. The Blackwall

Tunnel added to the area's tendency towards superlatives when it was opened by the London County Council in 1897, being the biggest underwater tunnel ever constructed at the time and costing a mighty £1.4 million – but it did nothing to improve the environment. By the time a second, parallel tunnel was opened in 1967 the whole area was nothing but traffic fumes, gas fumes, chemical emissions, and toxicity. Even though gas production stopped in 1976, an atmosphere of poisonous decay hung around the site – and it was this that the promoters of the Birmingham bid seized upon in their final submissions to the government. Who, they asked, would want to visit such a place, let alone live there in the new Millennium Village? Birmingham's site was clean, unused, untainted by the Victorian drive for profit. Greenwich was offering an inaccessible, industrial wasteland.

Yet Greenwich won through and, in retrospect, you can see why. At the time of the big decision, *The Times* wrote in an editorial, 'Greenwich has the right symbolic and practical credentials to host what ought to be the most important exhibition in Britain since 1851', and it was this symbolism, this overwhelming historical resonance, which finally tipped the balance in its favour. However suitable Birmingham might have been for a major international exhibition, it was not on the prime meridian, and could not claim to be the home of universal time. The emblematic significance of placing the exhibition at Greenwich was just too powerful to resist. What's more,

Birmingham couldn't offer anything like the variety of alternative attractions that London could – the museums, galleries, theatres, restaurants that make London (despite its glaring shortcomings) one of the great capital cities of the world, and that are waiting just upriver for anyone who makes the trek to see the exhibition and still wants more. So Greenwich was picked in early 1996.

The next thing was to clean up the old site – by that time, the property of British Gas – and start work on a millennium building and a decent transport network.

Building started in June 1997, when 8,000 concrete piles were driven into the ground and the foundations and main services were put in. By this time it was well known that the building was going to *be* a dome, and that it was the work, principally, of architects of the Richard Rogers Partnership, along with consulting engineers, Buro Happold. Rogers himself was already known for his design of the Pompidou Centre in Paris, and the new Lloyd's Building in the City of London. Both of these had created tremendous interest, as well as neatly polarising the population into those who thought him a genius and those who reckoned him a charlatan. So when the Dome plans first appeared – even though they weren't drawn by Rogers himself, but by Mike Davies in collaboration with Gary Withers of the design company Imagination – they generated controversy from the word go and gave newspaper cartoonists endless scope for fun at the Millennium Dome's expense. Anything to do with Rogers, it was felt, had to be worth a crack. What's more, a general election in May 1997 made sure that there was extra uncertainty just before construction began. Up to this point, it had been a Conservative government and a Conservative-sponsored idea. Would the incoming Labour government stick with the plan? They confirmed their backing for it shortly after taking over: another moment of anxiety dealt with.

But however much fun the critics made of the Dome – *because* it was a dome – its proponents argued that, in the circumstances, it was the best shape and the best overall approach. It had to cover a huge site, without being overweeningly massive itself. It had to provide all-year protection from the elements for whatever exhibits were to be installed. It had to be flexible: open enough to make room for just about anything. It had to have a very clear and empty floor plan. And it had to be reasonably priced and reasonably quick to assemble. The total budget for the Dome itself (including infrastructure and remedial works) of around £260 million sounds big; but a single conventional office block, occupying just a fraction of the space, can come in at £40 million without any difficulty at all; in fact, on a pound per square yard basis, the Dome costs about the same as the shed-like warehouses you find in modern retail parks. Nor does an office block or retail park usually have to be the focus of an entire nation's dreams and scepticism. Nor does it have to suffer unfavourable comparisons with Aalto's Finnish Pavilion at the

New York World Fair of 1939, to say nothing of Paxton's brilliant Crystal Palace for the Great Exhibition of 1851, or the Festival of Britain site of 1951.

Four months after work had started, the twelve yellow masts arrived ('Van Gogh cornfield yellow', to use the design parlance) and began to go up on the site. Each mast is nearly a 100 yards long, sits on a 30-foot steel pyramid in a reinforced concrete base, and to put the things up took one of the biggest cranes in Europe – which itself arrived from the continent on a fleet of twenty-four lorries. There's a nice hint of that forgotten Greenwich world of sails and sailing vessels in the way that the masts are held up by forestays and backstays; one of the construction team complained that trying to fit the sections of roof fabric in place on a windy day was 'like tying a sail down in a storm'.

But then, these construction workers were abseilers rather than sailors, eighty-two of them specially brought in to attach the one million square feet of Polytetrafluoroethylene (PTFE, or Teflon) covered glass fibre panels to the cat's cradle of wires stretched between the masts. They had to fix 144 separate panels, using 20,000 aluminium clamps, working clockwise around the Dome, starting at the top and making their way down to the base. The upper panels – the triangular-shaped ones, coming together around the Dome cap like segments of an orange – each weigh well over 1,500 pounds, but were relative lightweights to attach. The lower panels – nearly 40 feet wide at the base – tip the scales at a massive 4,000 pounds, and each took a team of fifteen men, plus a crane and two winches, to put up. The central ventilation cap is made of aluminium, and contains sixty different sections, computer-controlled to regulate the internal temperature of the Dome automatically. And that, too, had to be craned up through the middle of the Dome and then worked into place by hand. The abseiling team needed fourteen miles of rope to keep them all up there – but it had to be caving rope, rather than climbing or abseiling rope. Why? Because caving rope is pre-stretched, designed not to give if it's under constant load, whereas climbing rope is only put under stress for part of the time – the load mainly being taken by the rock face.

It took three months to get the high-strength support cables up, and another three months to install the roof panels. But in precisely one year the Dome, that shape laden with symbolism and significance, was up. And for anyone who had been watching the gradual construction of this building, it was an odd moment to realise that the thing was now more or less in one piece, that nothing more was going to be immediately visible from the far shore, or from the summit of Greenwich Park. It took a while to work out that the strange hole in the Dome's flank was for an existing air ventilation chimney emerging from the Blackwall Tunnel (surrounded by a concealing wall inside the Dome) and that there would be no more bits added on to the yellow masts – they were always going to look like enormous pieces of wicker. But the arrival of the finished Dome also made the point that the millennium event *was* actually going to happen. After all the debate about whether or not to have a Millennium Exhibition and, if so, where to have it and in what, the Dome became its own advertisement. Incredibly prominent, it had to announce its own success as it went up, or be condemned to two years' ridicule. The design structure announced its progress, attracted the world's attention, and then presented a perfect, finished exterior, twelve months after the task began. Instead of endless months of scaffolding, slowly growing steel frameworks, cladding and boring, we had a kind of circus act at the end of which – hey, presto! – a huge, complete building appears, bang on cue and just as the designers said it would. It became its own best promoter.

Inside, work was getting under way on the central arena, able to hold an audience of up to 12,500 people, and the 'Baby Dome' with a capacity of 5,000. There were one and a half miles of underground conduits to lay, carrying the electricity, water and gas services from the external supply pods grouped around the perimeter of the structure – not to mention a ten-foot-deep trench to allow performers access to the central area. There was also the question of air. With nearly 2.8 million cubic yards of air inside the Dome (the air weighs more than the skin of the Dome itself) plus a daily average of between twenty and thirty thousand people inside, how do you keep things fresh? Again, the fact that it's a fabric dome rather than a concrete building helps. Like any tent, it can use its own draughts to good effect: fresh air comes in around the edges, is treated as necessary (cooled or warmed – but not to office standards) and then leaves through the cap. This way, the entire volume of air inside the Dome can be changed once every hour. And yet, like any civilised tent or marquee, it responds sympathetically to the outside weather. Sunshine can penetrate the fabric; cooler or warmer weather can alter the nature of the experience within; you're not isolated from the world in some kind of airtight, characterless bubble. In the States, perhaps, you'd have to keep the weather permanently at bay – an extreme climate demands extreme solutions. But southern England still has a pretty temperate climate, and it's right not to exclude it from the encounter. Whoever first called the Dome a dustbin lid was going for a headline rather than a legitimate critique. Whether you call it a building, a tent, a structure or a concept, it is unarguably clever, memorable and not quite like anything else.

But what does it mean for Greenwich? After all, the Dome has a projected lifespan of twenty-five years. How will it fit in once the nervous excitement of the new millennium has calmed down?

The millennium experience's two great predecessors – the Great Exhibition and the Festival of Britain – enjoyed mixed fortunes. The Crystal Palace, built for the Great Exhibition, was an outstanding success, drawing some six million visitors. Indeed, it was such a hit that once the exhibition was over,

Paxton's 4,500-ton structure was moved from Hyde Park to Sydenham in 1854, to become the centre of an amusement park, accidentally renaming a part of south London. Unfortunately it was never quite the same once it left Hyde Park – losing its lustre, its dignity, and finally burning down in one of London's most spectacular blazes (the gutters ran with molten glass) in 1936. The Festival of Britain, which spread across the south bank of the Thames, offers a more hopeful parallel. This, like the Greenwich Dome, was put up on mainly derelict riverside land, and not only gave rise to the Royal Festival Hall, but also – in a curious prefiguring of the Greenwich millennium experience – offered a Dome of Discovery and an object called the Skylon: a kind of futuristic rocket shape, held in suspension in a cradle of steel wires, something like one of the masts supporting the roof of the Dome. The Festival was a great success, attracting eight million enthusiastic visitors at the height of post-war austerity – visitors so keen to enjoy themselves that even if the weather was bad (which it frequently was) they were prepared to dance outside in the rain, provided someone was prepared to play for them. Indeed, it was largely thanks to the Festival of Britain that the whole South Bank complex came into being – a complex which is now moving into a third phase, with a major revamp for the new century involving the National Film Theatre, the Hayward Gallery, the new IMAX complex and so on.

Will the same be true for Greenwich and its Dome? Will it

usher in a new cultural dynamic? Will it put Greenwich in the centre of the map, rather than leave it on the margins? If nothing else, the millennium celebrations have already brought in better communications than this part of south-east London has enjoyed for a long time – not since the great days of riverboat traffic has Greenwich been so accessible. And this has been managed largely without the kind of environmental insanity which gripped the Victorians (who seriously contemplated driving a railway line through the Queen's House) or the developers of the late 1960s with their Thamesmead motorway. What's more, any economic activity (and, one way or another, there's been plenty of that since the construction work began in 1997) can be said to be a good thing in a part of London which has missed out on many of the delights of late twentieth-century material investment. New buildings, new homes, new interest, the eager refurbishment of Greenwich's monuments and museums – all these are promising developments.

But does the Dome fit in? Can it be seen as the next in line to all the other great buildings and institutions which litter Greenwich? Yes: without being overly fanciful, you can argue that with its masts, rigging and sail-like roof, it summons up images of the maritime past which was once so central to this part of London. It wears its engineering on the outside, draws attention to the mathematics which holds the whole thing together and in that way hints at the geometrical patterns and arcane angles that Flamsteed and his successors so laboriously descried in the heavens. Like the Queen's House and the Royal Naval College, it's a building which has aroused fierce controversy, has alienated and delighted the public and the professionals, but – above all – has made its presence felt. And you can trace a meandering line of descent, from Duke Humphrey to Henry VII, to the Queen's House, to the Royal Observatory, to the Royal Naval College, to the National Maritime Museum and finally to the Dome – there because of the prime meridian and everything which brought *that* into being, the last word in that long history. You could say that it just about fits.

Will Greenwich revive in the twenty-five years that the Dome is due to stand? Will this latest development stop the rest of the city moving ever westwards and help to re-establish the east? After all, Greenwich has had to fight against gradual and persistent decline ever since the nineteenth century, with the closure of the big dockyards, the disestablishment of the Royal Naval Hospital, the encroachment of London's urbanisation. But if you combine all the attention generated by the millennium with the longer-term and more gradual economic revival on the north bank of the river, plus the latest redevelopments around Bermondsey and the Pool of London, could the east start to claw back some of its old vitality?

It always helps to have a symbol people can point to – even a controversial one, a symbol which arouses mixed feelings.

Docklands can gesture to Canary Wharf, once the great white elephant of the east, now a hub of commerce. Birmingham can point to the Symphony Hall – enormously expensive, called elitist and a misspending of public funds when it was going up, but now the city's most potent focus of pride and aspiration. It could just happen at Greenwich: the interest generated by one remarkable building can provide just the energy needed to change the way people see the rest of the place. The fortunes of Greenwich have been good, bad, sometimes inexplicable. The fact that so much is there, in so small a space, makes the whole area extraordinary. All it needs now is a bit of luck.

INDEX